*Dreaming in*

# LIBRO

*Dreaming in*

# LIBRO

## How a Good Dog
## Tamed a Bad Woman

## LOUISE BERNIKOW

A Member of the
Perseus Books Group

Chapter Two, "The Dog Is a Ham,"
appeared in a slightly different form in
*Dog Is My Co-Pilot:*
*Great Writers on the World's Oldest Friendship* (Crown, 2003).

Designed by Trish Wilkinson
Set in 12 point Goudy by the Perseus Books Group

Library of Congress Cataloging-in-Publication Data

Bernikow, Louise, 1940–
  Dreaming in Libro : how a good dog tamed a bad woman / Louise
Bernikow.
    p.  cm.
  ISBN-13: 978-0-7382-1096-4 (hardcover : alk. paper)
  ISBN-10: 0-7382-1096-X (hardcover : alk. paper) 1. Dogs—New
York (State)—New York—Anecdotes. 2. Bernikow, Louise, 1940–
3. Women dog owners—New York (State)—New York—Biography.
4. Human-animal relationships—Anecdotes. I. Title.
SF426.2.B484 2007
636.7092'9—dc22                                    2007007516

Published by Da Capo Press
A Member of the Perseus Books Group
www.dacapopress.com

Note: Some of the names and identifying details of people
associated with events described in this book have been changed.

Da Capo Press books are available at special discounts for
bulk purchases in the U.S. by corporations, institutions,
and other organizations. For more information, please contact the
Special Markets Department at the Perseus Books Group,
11 Cambridge Center, Cambridge, MA 02142, or call
(800) 255-1514 or (617) 252-5298, or e-mail
special.markets@perseusbooks.com.

10 9 8 7 6 5 4 3 2 1

For the next one

# Contents

*Prologue*                                              *ix*

1   Fish Out of Water                                     1

2   The Dog Is a Ham                                     33

3   City Slicker                                         59

4   Citidog at the Seashore                              93

5   Calamities                                          119

6   Doctor Libro Goes to Work                           147

7   Dreaming in Libro                                   175

8   All Messages Have (Not) Been Erased                 191

# Prologue

My mother always told me I would grow into my feet and my nose. Either she was mistaken or she downright lied because here I am grown up, all five feet three inches of me, and when I ask for size nine shoes, salespeople gape. But the shoes do fit. My nose is as prominent as it was when my mother said those dastardly or reassuring things to me and I doubt that my face is so much larger now. It's a prominent nose, the kind that the kindly say gives "character" to my face.

She also said I was allergic to dogs, which made sense at the time. Every whiff of dust or bit of goldenrod floating on a breeze sent me into paroxysms of sneezes, and a multitude of other things, from air pollution to anger, caused attacks of asthma. I was indeed a sensitive child, but my mother lied and she did so, I believe, for her own purposes. She didn't like animals—not that she had met many on the streets of suburban Queens—and she equated them with mess. With work, too, I suppose, since mess means work, as in cleaning up, to most people. I can't recall an opinion expressed by my hard-working father, so I imagine the issue never went far enough to be put to him. We had no "pets." Most people I knew had no pets either.

I grew up, got educated, and became a writer and a sophisticated urban type, fancying myself on the banquettes of cafés in the great cities of the world, cigarette in my mouth, literature and politics on my mind. I dropped the cigarettes eventually and did get to visit many banquettes in many places; but dogs, cats, chickens, horses, hamsters—the entire animal world—were no more than phantoms to me. I never saw them, never thought about them, never missed them, barely ever read about them. I considered the dogs and cats who lived with some of my friends' pieces of furniture, though they did move about. But what was there to say? When people began advocating for animal rights, I wanted to direct their attention to the suffering human beings I saw every day, sleeping in doorways and begging for food, physically and mentally afflicted, in need of help and having a right to it. When we've taken care of the people, I said, we'll do the animals.

Just when I'd settled into my own skin, thinking I knew who I was, what I believed, cared about and needed, everything went topsy-turvy. On a sunny late May afternoon, three years before the world entered a new millennium, I was jogging in Riverside Park at the edge of the Hudson River. My curiosity led me to stop on the path and elbow my way through a small crowd surrounding a police car. Elbowing my way through a crowd was a skill I had honed over the years, at large public demonstrations I had covered as a journalist or joined as a citizen. Being a small person helped. That afternoon, I wanted to see what the fuss was about. I always want to know what a fuss is about.

As I pressed my nose against the window of the police car, the brown creature curled in a ball on the back seat raised its head and became a dog with mesmerizing eyes. Amber they were, those eyes, not brown and somehow not as young as the rest of him seemed to be. He stood on spindly legs, nose against the glass, a stumpy tail wagging and those old eyes fixed on me.

So I took him home. It was the most daring thing I'd ever done and I was not a cowardly woman. I'd done many things that were, in hindsight, dangerous or foolish, with men I'd never met before or in countries that didn't think women should roam about on their own, or in gambling casinos where conventional wisdom dictated not another chip on the table, not another dollar in the pot. In my Fulbright fellowship year in Spain, I'd preferred flamenco dancing on tabletops in local bars to freezing my toes while doing research in the National Archives and, though it was now many years later, I'd make the same choice at the click of a castanet. Having no regrets made me a free spirit in my book and a "bad woman" in some other books. But taking the brown dog home was an act more impulsive and irrational than even I thought myself capable of.

Afterward, in the long afterward that became my life with this dog, people would praise my compassion. I had saved him from the killing chambers of the animal control people. I would be welcomed into the animal rescue community as a softhearted sucker or a saint, but I was neither. I don't know what I was, except that I simply wasn't myself.

We left together, with me holding the rope knotted to the beautiful brass-studded brown leather collar around the dog's neck. I was surprised that he followed along. Didn't he know that I carried a nightgown, birth control, and my passport in the trunk when I owned a car, ready to leave for Paris at a moment's notice? Why would a dog want to come home with someone like that? Hadn't anyone told him that I had no experience, zero idea what a dog *was*, much less how to care for one? Did he know or understand anything at all, or was he, too, simply not himself?

He was small, with a flat brown coat rippled by black lines, the color of maple fudge. On his chest was a flat white patch in the shape of Superman's insignia. His ears were floppy; his tail cropped or, as I thought of it that day, stumpy. Around his ankles were bands of white, not quite as high as kneesocks. His nose was squished flat on his face and he had those eyes.

I'd said I would "take" him, not keep him, I reminded myself as, tailed by members of the crowd that had been around the police car, our merry band walked south, up a flight of stone steps, across Riverside Drive and onto my street. One member of the accompanying crowd—the dog's fan club—offered to go to the pet store and buy a few provisions.

Being provisional was important. I might feed him or give him water. Maybe he could stay a night or two. I had no idea what I was doing, but the dog seemed to know what he was doing. He climbed the four flights of stairs in my building with a great deal of interest, even determination, though I noticed that one of his hind legs seemed stiff. I opened the apartment door. In the place I use as a writing studio, piles of books and papers were everywhere, including on the floor. While he investigated, I worried.

"Don't touch the books," I said. He kept sniffing.

Given the multiethnic nature of the neighborhood, it occurred to me that the dog might not speak

English. The only other language I knew well and, luckily, the most likely alternative was Spanish.

"*No toca los libros*," I shouted.

He looked at me with comprehension, though comprehension of *what* I could not tell. It might have been syntax. But he did not touch the books. And now he had a name: "Libro," which means book.

# 1

# Fish Out of Water

*We tend to think things are new
because we've just discovered them.*
—Madeleine L'Engle

I do love a mystery. Where the dog in the park had come from—his "backstory," as they say in Hollywood—was a puzzle worthy of Miss Marple or the BBC's Jane Tennyson. If someone had taken the trouble to train him as well as he turned out to be trained and adorn him with the beautiful brass-studded leather collar he was wearing when he followed me home, why abandon him? I imagined that he was a runaway, though he showed no signs of having been abused. I considered the possibility that his "person," elderly or

stricken with AIDS, had died. When an x-ray of his
right hind leg, which was slightly turned out and stiff,
revealed two steel pins, one from hip to knee and
another from knee to ankle, I had another idea. The
black-and-white image I stared at in the vet's office
showed a mercury-like river of steel running down
the leg, an expensive piece of mercury, representing
surgery costing over a thousand dollars. Perhaps his
"people" were among the hi-tech yuppies invading the
neighborhood whose "bubble had burst," as the finan-
cial pages said, and who, unable to pay for his upkeep,
had left the dog where someone would find him.

He was a boxer, the vet had said, probably a purebred
one. "Purity" meant little to me, certainly nothing to get
excited about. I dimly associated "purity" with Hitler's
passion for the Aryan race. I don't care much for pedigrees in people, either, and I preferred to think that
Libro, with his imperfect swaggering gait, had a bit of
Brooklyn about him.

After I'd done the requisite moral thing, walking
him uptown, downtown, and crosstown day after day,
discerning that no part of town seemed more familiar
than any other, posting "found" fliers on bus stops and
trees into the month of June, and receiving not a single
call, I decided that Libro's fate was truly in my hands.

Within weeks, I was sure that Libro had come from a
good home with attentive, loving people and that his

past included an affectionate relationship with someone who spoke Spanish and at least one black man. I
knew this because black men in the street elicited extra doses of Libro's attention and enthusiasm, which
were not always so welcome.

It also had to have been a city home. Libro knew
what cars were before we ever entered one together—
he stopped, of his own accord, at street corners, waiting
for my permission to cross. Cars were dangerous, but
they were also fun. If someone parked on the street, the
opening of the door as the driver disembarked from
the vehicle alerted Libro from as far as ten or twenty
feet away. He would pull me over and beg the poor
driver for a ride by sitting, wagging his tail, and becoming even more adorable. On Friday afternoons, when
cars were being packed up for the weekend, he per-
formed the same attempt at seduction. I wondered
what he would do if one of those daddies hefting cool-
ers and blankets into their car trunks, or mommies
folding up strollers, or handsome hunks lashing surf-
boards to their roofs said, "Sure, come along, Libro."

And he seemed entirely at ease with apartment
living. He went along naturally as we descended and
climbed four flights of stairs, up and down, home to
street, street to home, three times a day. Stairs were
the price I paid for living in an 1890s building full of
"character" and tradition. The building was also full
of neighbors who immediately made Libro, the only

canine resident, the center of attention. When the saxophone player, first floor rear, practiced, Libro lay on his doorstep, ears up. The second floor stockbroker and Libro spoke dogtalk together. Don't ask me. If Maria on the third floor was cooking *osso bucco* or *scaloppini a limone*, he tried to slide under her door, nose first. Sometimes, even when Maria was not cooking, Libro would stop, dig in and lie down to wait, in case she started again.

Those stairs kept me trim, though they annoyed delivery people, who arrived huffing and puffing with arms full of groceries or dry cleaning, holding me responsible for the lack of an elevator. "Well," I would say, aiming for apologetic, "some people pay a gym to work out on a Stairmaster, but you got it free," which rarely made me any friends. Libro made more friends than I did. When the downstairs doorbell rang, he ran to the door. As I opened it, he poked his head into the hallway and if the person with Chinese food or laundry didn't panic, he'd greet them. I took to telling the laundry to deliver the clean sheets and towels to "*la casa de Libro*," or "Libro's house," an address they came to know by heart.

Far more mysterious than Libro's origins or the perplexing question of what exactly a dog *was*—another conundrum—were the changes his presence caused in me. I, who had always snickered at grownups talking gobbledygook to what I assumed were bemused canines, heard language escape from my mouth that I didn't know was lurking there. "Sweetie pie" was the least offensive. I babbled like an infatuated nincompoop, which, indeed I was. A neophyte dog person in love, I had trouble yanking hard on his leash to correct his wanderings, which wise dog people advised, because it felt mean. I was astonished at his sweet temperament, but even more, I was amazed at *my* tenderness toward *him*. Perhaps what animal lovers really love is access to their own tenderness. This is important in cities like mine, where tenderness will usually guarantee that you don't get a taxicab on the street or a good seat at the movies. It might even get you killed.

The city, New York City in particular, has always drawn people from the provinces, as they were called, who wanted to escape the limitations and intrusiveness of small towns. Like Garbo, they merely "vanted to be alone." We inhabitants are known for, and pride ourselves on, what critics take for indifference but is actually respect for privacy. I live in the anonymity capital of the nation. You can be, especially in my neighborhood, transgender, transvestite, even transterrestrial or just plain weird, and hardly anyone bothers you. You can stay up all night painting a masterpiece, executing computer scams, or saving the world and nobody knows. Nobody gives you a second look if you travel the subway with a small piano on your back or come home at noon in last night's evening wear. I actually have a hard time at Halloween knowing who is wearing a costume.

But get a dog and your life is suddenly public property. Everybody comments. From day one of our life together, strangers in the street stopped to admire Libro, ask how old he was, and wonder where he slept at night. I still don't know why the latter intrigued them, nor whether they would have wondered if he had been female. They also asked if he was friendly, which, so far, he was. His yanking on his leash prompted clichéd remarks like "who's walking who?" Once he discovered that the leash could be used in a game of tug, he began to choose partners according to some system I could not fathom, carrying the leash in his mouth to offer to total strangers, most of whom were willing to grab it, though we did meet some wet blankets along the way.

"Does he bite?" asked a boy of about ten, coming down our block and heading for the park, decked out in soccer gear on a Saturday morning.

"Only if you bite him," I said. So far, that had seemed a safe prediction.

The boy approached, touched Libro lightly on the head, then withdrew his hand quickly—as if he had thrust it over an open flame—and bolted away down the street.

Early in our cohabitation, an admirer stopped us, praised Libro's good looks, got a saliva-covered hand for it and asked how long they live. By "they," he meant boxers, for he fancied himself a worldly fellow and knew that the life spans of dog breeds varied. How cruel a question. I told the sourpuss that whatever canine actuarial charts said, everything about Libro had already defied the odds, beginning with his discovery of an unlikely savior, namely me, and that I assumed he would continue to do so for a very long time.

The dog run in Riverside Park was full of more experts, and many of them were helpful to a neophyte dog person in love, afraid of making her poor guy feel rejected by correcting his behavior. I eagerly sought advice for curbing Libro's habit of greeting admirers with astounding athletic jumps onto his hind legs, often landing kisses on the mouths of humans who were nearly six feet tall. When asked what kind of dog he was, I had taken to saying he was a flying kissing dog. But he had already knocked the eyeglasses off the face of a small woman who stopped to pet him. The people in the dog run urged me to stop finding Libro's jumping so hilarious and showed me a technique that involved using my knee as a barrier to stop it.

Dangerous, I thought, especially for me. Besides, I am verbal. Words are my connection to the world. Because Libro sat and cocked his head intelligently when I spoke to him or perhaps simply because it was

my way, I thought that explaining things in a reasonable manner was all that was required: Don't touch
the books because you will tear them and I won't be
able to do my work and we both will starve. Don't
worry about the Republicans because they will soon
be gone. Feminism means treating women like human
beings. Did you know that a woman piloted a ship
around the Cape of Good Hope? And don't jump on
people, because you will scare the bejesus out of them.
Time would tell how far explanations would carry me.

I also had differences of opinion with other people
about slobber. I liked the gooey "kisses" with which
Libro covered my face. Others found it repulsive. It
was, I insisted, a good beauty treatment, like face
cream made from placenta.

Then, just when I was beginning to feel the small-
est bit of confidence that I knew what I was doing, I
had an encounter whose dissonance bordered on the
ontological. A woman walked past us in the street
pulling a suitcase on wheels. Libro not only barked at
the rolling object, but tried to lunge after it.

"Sorry," I said apologetically to the startled woman,
who stopped and leaned against a parked car for support, slightly breathless. "He thinks it's alive."

"*He* doesn't think," she snapped. "*You* think *for* him."

*I* think for him? What a concept! I thought my job
was to understand him much as I would have tried to
understand a visitor from a foreign country. In the

years to come, I would increasingly rely on intuition and observation to tell me how Libro operated, decoding his various postures, gestures, and sounds as clues to how he felt and what he wanted. Had he been an unruly menace, I might have thought differently, but Libro was so well behaved and cordial and he looked so wise, it had hardly seemed necessary to exercise much domination over him and certainly not to do anything as intrusive and imperialistic, in my book, as *think* for him.

Curious about how he experienced the world, including this strange woman who had taken him home, I was tempted to taste his food and biscuits, but I couldn't bring myself to try. I did, just once, get down on all fours beside him, partly for knowledge of his spatial perspective, but when the doorbell rang and he went to the door, I padded along, too. I wanted to experience the helplessness of being two feet off the ground with the doorknob three more feet above us.

"Where are the grownups, Libro?" I joked, with what I thought of as a beleaguered glance at the door we could not open.

Instead of joining my game, Libro looked at me sternly and a bit annoyed. When I resumed the upright position and did my duty by opening the door, he wagged his tail, approving, I supposed, of things being in their rightful places, order restored.

No, I couldn't think for him. The best I could do was navigate between received wisdom, other people's opinions and my own intuition, plus Libro's preferences insomuch as I could decode them. He and I would negotiate a way of being together that suited us both, whatever it looked like to outside eyes.

೧৩

When Memorial Day came around again, marking a year of living together, I decided to call it Libro's second birthday and gave him a party. I filled our home with neighborhood friends: Janet the lawyer, her husband Stan and their three-year-old beagle, Baxter; John the photographer who worked for the Parks Department and his mutt, Amber; Chen, the industrial designer and her ink black sharpei, who was Libro's age and with whom we had a standing date in the park mornings before nine, when off-leash frolic was legit. Unable to find maple fudge crepe paper to hang, I went for summer white, though the humans did get maple fudge ice cream. I placed liver treats and chew sticks in silver bowls on the floor of my studio and a big water bucket on the terrace. Move over, Martha Stewart!

Libro sat on the couch hunched in a corner. He glared at me. He tracked the "guests" in and out of the studio, the kitchen, the terrace, not more than a quarter inch from their tails. He never took his eyes off them. When one of the "guests" approached a treat bowl, too polite to growl but obviously wanting to, he turned and glared at me again. What had I done? Oops. I had forgotten that he was a dog.

I spent an entire summer, in what is arguably the greatest city in the world, basically tending the live-stock (Libro) and the agriculture (the garden).

Tending Libro was physical and intimate. Although shorthaired boxers require little grooming and Libro in particular was fastidious and catlike about his own per-sonal hygiene, I was still required to do certain things to his body. Not all of these were agreeable. He hated having a bath because he hated getting wet. I could not devise another way to do it. The sound of water running in the tub sent him to the other end of the apartment, where he planted his feet belligerently, dig-ging in, even though he was standing on an oak floor. He refused to move until my invitation became a sharp command. What I thought of as the delightful aromas of citrus or oatmeal doggy shampoo did not impress him. He stood with his eyes closed, tolerating the ap-plication of shampoo, the washcloth—I had been cau-tious about touching his "private parts" until mothers of boys told me to stop worrying—and the rinsing. When the end of the bath came, never soon enough, Libro leaped out of the tub and shook himself as though the water was pricking his skin. Towels were not welcome. He always soaked the floor.

His eyes-closed, I'm-putting-up-with-this-because-I-have-to bathtub look was even more intense when I cleaned his labyrinthine ears. The sight of ear cleaner and cotton pad sent him into exile until I gave up trying to explain that it wouldn't hurt, demonstrating with Q-tips in my own ears and assumed the uneasy role of "master"—"mistress" seemed too slutty—by insisting he participate.

His belly, which Libro eventually was willing to expose to me, had a ticklish spot halfway between his navel and his private parts. The first time I rubbed it accidentally, part of a general caress, I was startled by the way his four legs waved and jerked in the air with obvious pleasure. So I tickled him deliberately after that, but only in the privacy of our home. The only time I did it on the street—he'd rolled over onto his back as I was sitting outside my building talking to a neighbor—passersby looked alarmed. I felt compelled to assure them that nothing sexual was going on.

Massaging his spine made him sigh. Scratching behind his ears caused his tail to wag. Stroking his forehead and admiring the feline grace of his long, slow whole body stretches, I was reminded of how lack of touch has been proven to be the major deficiency in failure-to-thrive children. People living alone, especially older people living alone, speak, when they dare to, of the same lack. With Libro around and with sessions like these, no matter what else I did, I was in no danger of becoming a failure-to-thrive woman.

That was the livestock. The agriculture was a garden that does not touch the actual earth, existing, as it does, five stories into the sky—on a south-facing apron about nine feet wide and fourteen feet long attached to the fifth floor writing studio where I work. The space is large enough for a Weber grill, a table, four chairs, a white market umbrella, a chaise, and many large pots and wooden planter boxes. This Eden has always been my escape from and victory over the worst aspects of city life.

"*No toca los flores,*" I said in warning, the first time Libro went, nose first, onto the terrace.

Luckily, Libro, a city character himself, had no interest in African daisies, morning glories, or jasmine. Not once did he approach the railings with anything like suicidal or even adventuresome intent. He did try, often, to catch bees in his mouth to no avail and he did track any flying thing with beady eyes, ready to leap, but only rarely rousing himself from the chaise to do so.

The things growing there, from early May through October, if I was lucky, did not interest Libro, but they did interest me. I am a neophyte gardener, but a proud one. The opening of the first tangerine rose of summer was heraldic; the last basil faltering in the fall elegiac.

One season, I had only white flowers; another, purple and red. Chives and oregano not only thrived, but threatened to strangle their companions. A foot-high evergreen bought in Vermont and potted and repotted every few years had now become a five-foot-tall tree in the largest pot possible, taking gracefully to strung lights in the wintertime. Over the years, I had begun to learn the difference between annuals and perennials, adapting to a cycle of loss and return, noticing that some things died and did not come back while others surprised with resurrection for no apparent reason. Things thrived when I paid little attention to them or might die even with the utmost care.

Though I don't think he learned any such philosophical lessons, Libro was consistently interested in the grill and the chaise. The grill, of course, because food was often on it, the aroma of sizzling beef or chicken drawing him like a hypnotist's swinging pendulum. The beef, chicken, fish, or vegetables dripped into the pan below, along with charcoal ashes. If I didn't watch carefully, I'd catch him with his face in the pan. When he looked up, startled, usually by a shout from me, he was a parody of minstrelsy—dark face smeared in white ash and a huge grin. But I did watch carefully.

The sturdy white chaise with its thin blue cushion was Libro's "place" when company came for meals *al fresco*. Although I was legally what the Census Bureau calls "single," I was hardly solitary. During our first year together, Libro had attracted a man who lived with a dachshund and we had, for a while, been a funny kind of family, but it hadn't lasted very long. I learned an important lesson from that debacle: just because a man is nice to his dog doesn't mean he is a nice man.

So yes, there were "men in my life" as Libro turned two, just as there was air in my life and fun in my life, but the male people were friends, not potential daddies for my pup. Roland the dreadlock-draped astrologer and entrepreneur was Libro's special buddy, in part because Roland is one cool dude and in part, I came to believe, because Roland, being a black man, reminded Libro of people he'd known before he got "lost" in the park.

An extensive circle of "aunties" came for lunch, dinner, or iced tea in the afternoon. Julie, working on her play about a nineteenth-century woman who piloted a ship around the Cape of Good Horn, was within visiting distance on the Upper West Side. Libro knew Elizabeth Cady Stanton's great-granddaughter, a foundation president, a female judge, and many writers. You would probably call most of the women writers "bad women," for they, like me, were ambitious, smart-talking, rebellious, and wished they had lived in Virginia Woolf's Bloomsbury or the bohemian feminist enclaves of Greenwich Village of the 1920s. Unfortunately, Heather lived on Long Island, where Poco, her

Dalmatian, actually had two mommies, and Libro would have to wait for the pleasure of getting to know them.

"Get on the chair," kept Libro away from the sizzling grill and the diners at the table, preventing that million-watt charm from even revving up in the hope of "people food." When we were alone, he and I, the chaise was "our place," usually at sunset, for what I thought of as a vaccination against failing to thrive. As the sun went down over the Hudson River and the windows of apartment buildings around us turned ruddy, he would lick my face, snuggle against me, sit up on my lap while I kneaded his spine, and sometimes sniff my bare toes.

∾

Every woman who walks a city street walks in the footsteps of a history that says she should not be doing so without a man by her side. For centuries, solo strolling invited suspicions of prostitution ("street walking") and could land a woman in jail. Even now, a female alone is not quite safe. She is potential prey, and if "something happens" to her, "something" like rape or murder, even in centers of enlightenment like New York City, one of the first questions asked, not too *sotto voce*, is this: "What was she doing out by herself?"

Libro freed me from whatever shadows of history stalked my own footsteps. With him by my side, I explored the neighborhood and the city, day or night, as I had never dared do before. With him, I had already met—or, rather, Libro had met and I had benefited from—more than a hundred people I did not know before, including doormen, building custodians, mail, UPS and FedEx people, shopkeepers, shoppers, pedestrians, drivers, and delivery people from the local dry cleaner's, laundry, and restaurants.

More than being released from fearing Jack the Ripper lurking in the shadows, I did not have to be going shopping, as women before me had done, to justify my prolonged presence in "public space." I was not a woman wandering about "suspiciously" alone; I was walking my dog.

I was a woman walking her dog at a dangerous time, night, in what had been a dangerous place, along Riverside Drive, where homeless people made the benches their beds. If any bench people were prone, Libro nuzzled them and it was my job to say, "He just wants to be sure you are all right." This was considered acceptable, even welcome, even to those dead drunk or heroin high, who used to scare me. Libro acquired a posse. Some began to harbor presents for him, like T-shirts lifted from garbage cans. He got a Mt. Holyoke College shirt from a bearded man who had saved it because, he said, Libro looked like an educated dog.

Month after month, season after season, we came to know every inch of our street, with its white granite townhouses now converted to apartments, their window boxes overflowing with vinca vines and red geraniums, much like the *balcones* of Madrid in summer, their windows blinking Christmas tree lights and their doors sporting wreaths when it snowed. Libro lifted his leg almost compulsively at each tree along the block until, having held her tongue for a year, one of my ecologically astute neighbors said timidly that she believed dog pee kills trees. I was abashed.

Now and then, he ran into other kinds of trouble. Oblivious to Libro ambling along one afternoon, a cat sat in the ground floor window of a building close to West End Avenue, preening and emitting a sound that must have been to the dog what the Sirens were to Odysseus. Felines could instantly turn Libro into a predator. This information added to my ever-expanding scenarios about his previous life: the chilling possibility that he had been trained for dogfighting, where cats are often used as bait. At any rate, cats were to him what catnip was to them.

He had war, not love, on his mind and in spite of his leash, in spite of me, rushed to the window, went up on his hind legs and tried to grab the cat, who was protected by a window screen. She, faster than the speed of light and faster even than he, disappeared. Libro was left pawing at the screen. He got down on the ground again on all fours and surveyed the premises.

I watched him strategize. He looked carefully at the now empty window, back at the street, then at the entry door to the building that housed the cat. It was a good twelve feet from where we were standing. He looked at the window again—perhaps the cat had forgotten about him and returned? No such luck. So he moved in the direction of the building's front door. Luckily, he didn't have a key.

Day or night, I avoided Broadway, the busiest, most commercial street in the neighborhood. Known to dog people as "the Broadway buffet," the street was always laden with the mysterious detritus of urban life. Not just boxes of half-gnawed Kentucky Fried chicken pieces or chocolate-covered candy-bar wrappers, both of which might kill Libro, but single sneakers flung in the street, abandoned baby carriages, stacks of old books and magazines and condoms, all of which I thought it better to avoid.

My favorite spot was Straus Park, an oasis of benches and plantings where West End Avenue and Broadway divide. Midday, the benches were filled with nannies of color minding young white children, rocking the carriages and strollers while catching up on news from home. Before the mayor's campaign to "clean up" the city, Straus Park had been a haven for people who slept outdoors year round. Now they only slept on the benches during the day.

Straus Park was erected as a memorial to Isidor and Ida Straus, who sank with the Titanic in the Atlantic Ocean in 1912. This disaster occurred at the height of American women's fight for the vote and because the lasting cry from the listing ship was the traditional maritime "women and children first," it became grist for antisuffrage forces. The antis peppered the news-papers of the day with finger pointing about the weak-ness of women and their need for special protection. This "privilege" somehow translated into an argument for keeping females out of the dangerous area of public life and citizenship. Mrs. Straus was hailed as the paragon of good womanhood, giving up her life to stand by her man or whatever position she was in when she refused to leave Isidor.

While Libro drank from the marble fountain, nan-nies clutched at their charges and barefoot men snoozed on the benches, I thought about good and bad women.

I was the adolescent who had identified with James Dean in *Rebel Without a Cause*, not Natalie Wood. I wanted to ride motorcycles with Marlon Brando in *The Wild Ones*—not with my arms around his waist, but gunning my own bike—and be on the road with Jack Kerouac. Beyond adolescence, I had turned my back on, or freed myself from, what my favorite phi-losopher, Lily Tomlin, called the world of "meatballs and mending." Although I was never quite as bad as the former boyfriend who thought it simpler to place unfinished food in the refrigerator still on its plate with the silverware atop it, ready for the next bites, I had to admit I would probably never win the Good Housekeeping Medal of Approval.

Therefore, I was an imperfect guardian—not "owner," a term I detest. Although the law considers dogs "property," I do not. Nor was I Libro's "mommy," for a myriad of reasons, beginning with the fact that he was a dog and I was not. I preferred to think of myself as his trusted friend, but there was no getting around the fact that in spite of my "bad woman" preferences, I had certain responsibilities to fulfill and skills to learn. As usual, I made mistakes.

If, inhibited by vanity, I didn't have my eyeglasses with me at the pet store, I might buy cat food instead of dog food, similarly packaged. If I forgot that the pet food stores in the neighborhood closed early on Sundays, I had to improvise. I could always buy generic dog food in the supermarket, but Libro had a "delicate" diet that addressed the common boxer affliction of colitis. So there were, I admit, a few Sunday nights with no food at the ready and rather than let the situation become a Dickens novel, I became Marie Antoinette—"Let them eat biscuits!" A whole bowl full of biscuits! When the store opened Monday morning, we were on the doorstep, hungry.

A few times, I forgot I had a dog. A movie with a friend, then dinner, then a stroll, and then . . . oops. An afternoon in the library deep in research and . . . *uh oh*. The dog people said Libro probably just slept while he waited at home for me, but I rushed back propelled by guilt. Bad woman. All he did was jump on me and lick my face while I waited for a reprimand that never came, except in my own mind.

&#x2619;

When our second winter arrived, I built a snow dog on the terrace. Not a bad one. Libro padded distastefully through the drifts that had accumulated and actually stopped to inspect my creation. He sniffed its somewhat abstract paws and ears, its solid body and proclaimed it fake, turning his back and loping into the warmth of the great indoors.

Contemplating gifts for Chanukah, Christmas, or Kwanza, I surveyed the acquisitions that accompanied my new life: a fluffy blue doggy bed, several ceramic water bowls, many toys in all genres, from plush to ropy, a fine leather leash, eye, ear, and teeth cleaners, plus a new wardrobe for me, suitable to my life as a "dog person." A ragtag assemblage of pants, tops, and shoes that could be discarded after the park (and after the dogs had their way with them) came from local thrift shops. Although I was still gaga with the excitement any lucky honeymooner sustains, years of watching the shekels stayed with me and I did notice what it all cost.

I live in a place where people with staggering amounts of disposable income have dogs and cats who go to salons and spas, ride in their own taxis, get draped in ermine and custom-made jackets, sport jewels on their collars, and have their portraits painted. Not my style. Nor, I didn't think, Libro's. He seemed egalitarian, if not downright proletarian—devoted to simple pleasures like eating, sleeping, playing, and loving. Neither of us was much of a frou-frou.

Still, we needed a roof over our heads and food for my table and his bowl, so I had begun doing what writers do, turning my life into material. First, I'd written a magazine article about the initial shock of living with Libro. He'd gotten his first taste of celebrity when the article—with a full-page color photograph—appeared. We traveled by taxi to the Condé Nast building downtown, where a "Visitor" tag on a chain was draped around his neck. We rode an elevator to a publication party in his honor, where he was deluged with dog treats by the magazine staff. He loved the spotlight and the treats.

It made perfect sense that my dog would have such a party. I was, after all, not only a media professional, but the person who had always said that if there were ever a shadow cabinet, I would like the post of Mistress of the Revels. I do love festivities and rituals; and Libro, by nature or by osmosis, appeared to do the same.

What else was there to do after that but write a book?

"You're writing about *what?*" my father said on the telephone.

He had been living alone for the two years that had passed since my mother's death and I worried about him as much as he did about me. This is how we love one another in my family. I had an indelible image of him pacing the floor of the condo in the hours after my mother's funeral, jangling the coins in his pocket incessantly. My parents had been married for nearly sixty years. There was something about the coins—as though he could buy back happiness—and the fact that Libro had appeared shortly before the first anniversary of my mother's death that I thought I should pay attention to, decipher the meaning of, but meaning eluded me. It was all metaphor.

"The dog."

The telephone line between New York City and Fort Lauderdale, Florida was silent. My father had been my biggest supporter since the days of bringing pens, pads, notebooks and magazines home for me from his candy store. But as I got older and it became clear to him that I was not going to marry someone who would provide a roof over my head—or a swimming pool—he worried. I could hear him thinking in the silence down there in his retirement village, trying not to patronize me, trying, as I'd taught him to do, to refrain from telling me what to do. A *dog* book? My university-educated, literary, brilliant daughter?

I jumped in to save him.

"Well, not really about the dog. About *me*."

"Oh, that's better. A memoir."

"Right. A memoir."

Contrary to all laws of physical geography, Libro insisted on being a semi-lapdog while I sat at my desk writing at the computer while chives popped up in the garden, thrived and withered again with the first frost. His hind legs planted on the floor, the rest of his sixty-five pounds stretched across my lap while I reached over his back to compose on the keyboard. If he got restless or bored, which he often did, he would hoist his entire body onto my lap, tuck his legs under him and sit up. This blocked my view of the screen and prevented further work.

When words emerged, I read them to him and he wagged his tail or he sighed. Usually, I resisted taking these as editorial comments. If I couldn't remember the width of his dark muzzle or the light in his amber eyes, I had only to look down at my lap. About halfway through writing the book about a woman like me adapting to a dog like Libro, the canine on my lap started to look different. Physically different, not just more familiar. Still tigerish in his movements, dainty-footed, long-tongued. Still amber-eyed and intense. But his body changed virtually overnight. The white patch on his chest had expanded; it appeared helium-inflated. If I hadn't known better, I would have said his chest was puffed with pride, but I did know better: he had developed the muscularity of an adult boxer. He was merely growing up.

In my wilder days, writing had been the outcome of inspiration, but as I mellowed and noticed that no knight was stepping forward on the first of the month with a rent check in hand, I had settled in to writing as actual work, nine to five, all week long and sometimes on weekends. Libro helped, not only by sitting for his verbal portrait, but by filling the solitude of my writing space with his breathing, tail-wagging, sighing, even the diversion of blocking the screen.

I am not the first to have this kind of help. Behind every productive woman writer, I am tempted to say, there is a great dog.

⁊

Emily Dickinson described to her mentor, Thomas Wentworth Higginson, how she found companionship in what others considered an isolated life: "Hills, sir, and the sundown, and a dog as large as myself that my father bought me. They are better than beings, because they know, but do not tell."

Across the Atlantic, at approximately the same time, Emily Brontë lived with a mastiff who, judging from the drawings she made of him, looked a lot like Libro. "Keeper," the first in an animal-saturated family to be allowed to live indoors—the first "house dog" in Haworth parsonage—was Brontë's steady companion on long walks across the moors, but as her friend Ellen Nussey wrote, she treated him "with the sort of feelings usually reserved for human beings." One of her last acts before dying was to feed Keeper.

Jane Welsh Carlyle had an equally affectionate and even more imaginative relationship with Nero, a small Maltese mix. She often took to writing letters signed by "Nero."

Unlike the others whose lives shadow mine and Libro's, Virginia Woolf's most important dog was female. The golden cocker spaniel named Pinka, a gift from Woolf's occasional lover, the writer and accomplished dog breeder Vita Sackville-West, was the model, literally, for *Flush*, a novel in which Woolf imagines the lives of Elizabeth and Robert Browning through the consciousness of their dog. Pinka modeled, literally, for the book's frontispiece. Among the effects of Flush's presence in the Browning household was the lifting of Elizabeth's long depression, her increasing awareness of her own strength after years of invalidism. But Woolf, no sentimentalist she, brilliantly painted the gaps in understanding between these two companions. Flush, in particular, was confounded by Miss Barrett's motivation in spending "hour after hour passing her hand over a white page with a black stick."

Perhaps the fictionalized poet ought to have explained what she was doing. I do believe that Libro, perhaps with some genetic memory of the canine muses before him, understood what I was up to. At the very least, he learned to respond to the words "I am working" by patiently settling down on my lap or the floor, ready to listen quietly if I wanted to communicate, even to be called to such duty if he was napping.

Not only do dogs know but not tell, as Dickinson said, but they also listen and do not speak. Libro's wordlessness was an antidote to the verbiage spinning ceaselessly from radio, television, other people, and my own brain. Mute he may usually have been, though barks and whines escaped him often, but he was far from expressionless. Eye contact was my second language and his first. In this way, dogs have been less troublesome to writers than children have, if accounts of constant interruption and demand are to be believed.

Still, a dog can be a nuisance to a wordsmith hard at the task. That very same Pinka, in her first weeks with Virginia and Leonard Woolf, was reported to Sackville-West as having "destroyed, by eating holes, my skirt, ate L's proofs and done such damage as could be done to the carpet." While Libro's presence was welcome while I was working most of the time, there were occasions when it was not, though I must say he never ate proofs or damaged carpets.

At exactly five every afternoon by his infallible internal clock, Libro jumped off my lap and boxed my leg to remind me it was dinnertime. If I was too mercifully hypnotized by a paragraph to stop working, I'd ask him to wait. But Libro knew better than I about what Maslow called the hierarchy of needs, in which food comes way before literature. Surely enough, one day he took himself to the kitchen, where, in a rational world, his needs were met at five in the afternoon. In the quiet, I went on with the paragraph, ignoring, in the throes of creativity, a peculiar scraping sound.

A paw punched my leg. Libro had used his nose to push the food bowl across two rooms and there it was at my feet, the wily dog looking at me intently.

"Yo! Forget something?"

Good God and Hell's Bells, Libro, I thought. Did Dickinson, Carlyle, or Woolf let their dogs determine their writing schedules? I hoped not. Did Emily Brontë let her mastiff interrupt her?

"Why don't you lie down and pretend your name is Keeper?"

I quickly retracted that. I would not wish Libro to be Keeper, who witnessed Emily's death and attended her funeral, as Mrs. Gaskell, the first Brontë biographer, tells it:

> Keeper walked in the short cortege of Charlotte, Anne, the servants and Mr. Brontë, behind the wooden coffin. He was taken into the church and the Brontës' own pew, where he sat quietly while the burial service was read. And for the next week he lay outside Emily's bedroom and howled.

It is an odd failing of historians and biographers that the presence of a dog in a writer's life goes largely unnoticed by them. "It's only a dog," they say, a dismissive non-observation that has led, for example, to Virginia Woolf's *Flush* being the most disdained among her novels. Yet for me and, I suspect, other female writers, the dog has occupied the place formerly inhabited by the mythological figure of the Muse, who is always configured as female. If inspiration and support for male writers has come from benevolent, maternal, sometimes sexy, female Muses, what then has it been for women? I say the dog. I say that "scribbling women," to use Nathaniel Hawthorne's phrase, have always needed an imagined audience that is neither critical nor derisive, a recipient of what Emily Dickinson called her "letter to the world/that never wrote to me" and that answers Gertrude Stein's question: "Who will say 'yes' to me?"

Libro said *yes*. "Only a dog" said *yes*, day and night, every week, month and year. And to him I said, for better and for worse, in sickness and health, and in the spirit of Molly Bloom: *yes*, *yes*, and *yes*.

# 2

# The Dog Is a Ham

*Fame is a fickle food/Upon a shifting plate.*
—Emily Dickinson

By the time he was a devastatingly mature four-year-old, Libro had been transformed from local heartthrob to incorrigible media hound. Publication of my first book about our life together, *Bark If You Love Me*, drew an interesting crowd to a grand gala on a September evening. The party was held in Riverside Park, close to the spot of our mutual rescue and near the dog run. The invitees included a twelve-year-old named Charlotte, a friend's daughter. Previously, her mother had regaled her, perhaps as a bedtime story, with the unfinished story I was writing: a woman finds a dog in the park and he comes to live with her; one day she meets a man who also has a dog and they all have a good time together until the man turns out to be a liar and a bad man. So the man is a dog, while the dog is a perfect gentleman and the woman is not sure what to make of that.

"I know," Charlotte had piped up, "the woman marries the dog."

And so I had, to all intents and purposes. Libro had not only moved permanently into my apartment, but also into the place called Significant Other in my life. Before Libro, my idea of a good time had been driving through the Khyber Pass on Labor Day weekend, which I did, or going up Benedict Canyon on a magazine assignment to interview a movie actor and not emerging for a whole week, which I also did. I always liked Gloria Steinem's answer to persistent questions about why she did not marry: "I do not breed well in captivity." For myself, I would have amended it to "I do not *breathe* well in captivity." Although I had come of age in an era defined by the slogan, "a woman needs a man like a fish needs a bicycle," I was coming to believe that a woman needs a dog like a fish needs the ocean.

By the time Libro decided I was his Person and he was my dog, the era that had given rise to phrases like Steinem's was three decades behind us. We had all survived the backlash of the 1980s, the postfeminist, postmodernist chill of the 1990s, and were now in the amnesia-doused, the-women's-movement-never-really-happened new century. Just when I'd worn myself out asking why there were so few women delivering serious news on television—or why there was no serious news on television—and what it really meant that so many educated "free" women were choosing diapers and strollers and saying "mommy track" instead of "social justice," a little brown canine had wedged his way into my life. By then, my wilder adventures were starting to be filed in the "been there, done that" category. So I was, though I hardly knew so at the time, ready for him.

And I was ready, I suppose, not only for tenderness, but for a measure of silliness, even treacle. Invitations to Libro's book party had gone out with terminally cute locutions like "Roberta Sklar, Sondra Segal and Creampuff" or "Molly O'Neal and all her dogs." I invited dog people who had never been to a book party and book people who had never been to a dog party. Marveling at how Libro was amalgamating the different parts of my world, I sat back to see what would happen.

Among the guests of honor was Eddie the mailman, or *Eduardo*, as his Dominican mother must have named him, who was always *hablando con Libro en español* as he pushed his cart down the street. Eddie came to the party in uniform, either having finished his route too late to change into civvies or because he wanted to be sure everyone knew that he was *the mailman* in the published book.

Among the guests, there were also a smattering of local politicians whose acquaintance I had made because Libro's needs—especially the need to run free at times with his friends in the verdant ribbon of Riverside Park—had awakened me to the fact that laws governing canines in our town had been drawn up more than a half century before. People who lived with dogs, intent on bringing legislation in line with modern living, had become a political force in the neighborhood and the city. With decades of political experience behind me, it was to be expected that I would join up. I was as passionate as ever about resisting oppression, but my immediate needs had shifted. I was at the age where I might have marched under the protest sign I saw on the Washington mall that read: "Post-menopausal Women Nostalgic For Choice." Although I no longer needed access to abortion or the morning-after pill, I myself defended every woman's right to her own reproductive choices; but personally, I didn't need an abortion, I needed a large, friendly, accommodating dog run. And a book party, with dogs.

A hundred party guests, dog people and book people, divided like two mismatched families at a wedding, watched the sun set beyond the volleyball courts into the Hudson River, chomped on hot dogs and listened to the even hotter rock and rollers in the Alpha Dog band. As Libro had already lifted the curtain for me on the unseen world of animal-human connections in the big city, he had also gallantly escorted me into a community of people like those who made up the Alpha Dog band, local musicians concerned with saving four-legged strays from the death chamber. Little did it matter that *he* had rescued *me* from an erratic, profligate, and promiscuous life. That was our secret.

It was no secret, however, that several former heartthrobs showed up for the party and I paid them no mind because I was in love with Libro. My new beloved behaved better than he had at his birthday party. He was willing to share the space with Creampuff the Maltese, Wally the Golden Retriever, Barclay, and his other pals, as well as dogs whose names I never got. Libro sat readily for photographs, although those more amateurishly taken came out with spots of red in his eyes, which made him look more like the devil than the star he was that night. But he turned out to be a poor dance partner, which I had always considered a disqualification in a love interest. Although he complied chivalrously when I lifted his forelegs to shake, rattle, and roll in time to the band, he winced. I'd forgotten, again, not only that he was a dog, but one with steel pins in his body. Gimpy legs do not a Fred Astaire make. For that, I'd have to keep looking.

"You're really going to love going on a book tour," I promised Libro, "starting with the plane, but first you have to practice getting into your little house."

By then, I knew a bit about things canine—including airplane travel—because Libro's entry into my life had come trailing an expanding number of people with information about dogs, along with websites and not a few e-mail lists, national and local, to fill in any gaps. I turned to the community of those who knew. Although naysayers abounded—people who would never let their beloved animals travel in the cargo hold of a plane from one spot of land to another—I had little choice if the adventure was to proceed. Had he been a dainty Maltese, Libro could have flown in the passenger cabin in a carrying case like a slotted shoebox, but weighing in at close to seventy pounds and thirty-something inches long, my guy needed a travel crate. I borrowed one from Matteo, his large male Portuguese pal, who lived three blocks away and had used the crate only twice.

Amber eyes enlarged and nostrils flared as Libro contemplated the potential torture chamber, assembled from its eight separate pieces into a gray metal whole with a mesh door that swung open and, unfortunately for him, closed. It sat for a dry run on the floor of my writing studio with his fleece blanket inside for familiarity and comfort, followed by a liver treat, for inducement.

"Inside, Libro. Go into your little house."

He went in. He lay down. I told him what a good dog he was, which he understood, and a very good sport, too, which fell on deaf floppy ears as he devoured the treat. Then I closed the hinged door and immediately he was standing up, nose against the grid, alarmed but not barking. He pawed at the door, politely at first, then frenetically. I stood my ground or, rather, sat it, close up against my imprisoned pup, murmuring words of encouragement, promising untold delights ahead if he would just tolerate the means of transport to them.

We practiced for a week.

By then, I had published eight books and gone on eight book tours. I knew how to make sure that there actually were books to sign and sell wherever we went, talk in sound bites, repeat the sound bites, get the book's title into every sentence, pack a solid-color, mix-n-match wardrobe, intensify eyeliner for television, and take it like a woman when only three people showed up for an event. I explained all this to Libro, whose new Italian leather leash, I told him, was a "dress up leash," and not to be chewed on, as dress up clothes were not be slobbered on and made up faces were not to be smothered with gooey kisses. Fame comes with a price. I'd bought a dog paw rubber stamp—generic, to be sure, but more experienced folk had nixed my plan to have him dip his actual paw onto a pad and sign books himself. Toxic, they said. Attention span problems, too.

"Just keep smiling. Wag your tail. Don't worry if they get your name wrong—we know it's not the astrological sign Libra, but let it go if people insist on telling you they too were born in October, ok? Don't correct them, no matter how dumb the comments are. Most people who interview us won't have read the book. Just be yourself. No barking. No peeing. No shoplifting."

That last instruction was necessary in spite of the fact that Libro's shoplifting—at a bookstore north of the city—had amused the audience, which, miraculously, numbered more than three. We'd assumed our positions—I at the lectern, book open, Libro flat on the floor, water bowl nearby. (He had a few requirements, after all.) Halfway through page ten—where I tell him I've never known a dog before and haven't a clue how to manage if he really wants to live with me—Libro rose languidly and started to wander away. The store manager met my alarmed eyebrows with a permissive wave. I read on. Libro disappeared down an aisle. At the top of page fifteen, he returned—with a stuffed toy in his mouth! A black and white, six-legged thing that I took to be an octopus, but turned out to be a lemur. He trotted up and offered me the toy for a game of tug. The audience roared.

What a showman. But I already knew that. We'd begun our promotions at the top of the media food chain, with a television network interview. The very spiffy, clever producer placed us in side-by-side winged back armchairs. Libro was as relaxed as though he'd seen bright lights, cable wires, cameras, interviewers, and producers all his young life. The camera moved in on me: "I'd have to say he opened my heart . . ." Soupy, I know, and exactly the kind of verbal pap I disdain, but true. Libro looked over, moved to the edge of his chair, leaned over, rested his head on my shoulder and let out the most audible, perfect, TV-moment sigh. Uncoached. Honest.

Television lights phased him not, nor would microphones in radio stations or cameras. As we spent November traveling in planes, trains, and automobiles to bookstores, television studios, and pet boutiques, I increasingly came to feel like Jackie Kennedy with the glamorous Jackie in Paris—I was just the person who escorted Libro Pumpernickel Pegleg Bernikow to the show.

I deserved little credit for anything Libro was or did. He seemed so entirely his own dog—gentle and smart, soulful and sweet, disciplined enough, eager and alert, all from the day he followed me home. But the "ham" in him, the ease with which he took to pitch-perfect performing and the extent to which he seemed to like it—had I anything to do with that?

Surely nobody taught stage presence or poise when he was in the whelping box. I had to admit I might have had some influence there.

A writer's work is necessarily alone work, sometimes happily solo, sometimes lonely. My niece, when young, once asked to visit me for Take Our Daughters to Work Day and as carefully as I explained there was nothing to see, she did come to stare at me as I sat at the desk, tapping the keyboard, scratching my head, getting some water and speaking to no one. And although I am at peace with the work I do and the only conditions under which I know how to do it, I am also the person who, age nine, practiced being Miss America in front of the Philco television set with a tablecloth for a cape and a candlestick for a scepter. I do love show biz. I do find the visibility—as opposed to the writer's sweatpants-clad invisibility—and the camaraderie exhilarating. More than that. The first television appearance I ever made—long before Libro was born—left an admiring friend saying, "The reason you are so good on TV is that when the little red light comes on the camera, you want to suck it." And so I did. And so did Libro.

Fresh from the triumph of the television taping in New York, I packed for our trip to California, northern and southern. My bag: wardrobe for several climates and appearances, makeup, vitamins. Libro's bag, a waterproof green and white beach tote with pockets and zippers: dress-up leash, treats, vitamins, and a small bag of food to tide him over after we arrived. As suggested by Matteo's experienced human travelers, I plastered the travel crate with neon-inked signs that had my name, flight, and seat number—lest he be mistakenly put on a plane to Kalamazoo and picked up by a drug lord—and then I disassembled the crate for easier transport to Kennedy airport.

A dog of Libro's size was hard to ignore inside the airline terminal, and the attention he drew was not always admiring. Some people, quite terrified, simply glared at me or moved away, sacrificing their places in the check-in line.

"Don't pee on anything," I said, wrapping his leash around my hand and giving him no more than six inches breathing space.

"Don't jump on anybody." My efforts at curtailing Libro's overaffectionate behavior, too often accompanied by liquid emanations from his slobbery mouth, had come to nought.

We were not exposed to the traveling public for long. As his vet had suggested, I fed Libro a tranquilizer while a porter reassembled the crate and I muttered silent homage to single mothers for all they juggle. I was relying on the kindness of strangers and very large tips. Libro got into his little house willingly, if a little suspiciously, and disappeared on the porter's handcart. I

watched him go with a tight heart. I bothered every airline employee, from the gate agent to the flight crew—
which happily included a sympathetic person who
lived with a German shepherd—to the captain about
Libro's safety down in the cargo hold until I wished I
had a tranquilizer myself. So, I'm sure, did they.

My beautiful dog staggered out of the crate in the bag-
gage claim area of the San Francisco airport like a dog
on an acid trip, eyes rolling, legs shaking. I got down
on my knees and threw my arms around him. He peed.
I cried. He peed again, this time hitting a suitcase
waiting to be claimed. I summoned two porters and escaped the terminal, finding a taxi and cradling him on
my lap—mercifully peeless—on the ride into the city.
Together we collapsed on the bed in our small, charming "dog friendly" hotel room. Luckily, I'd insisted on a
day's recovery time before hitting the hustle. It had
been easier to get concessions to the "special needs" of
a dog on tour than for a mere human author, whose desire for rest or transition days was usually seen by tour
schedulers as a waste of money and the mark of a diva.
    After a snooze, we wandered down Polk Street to
Union Square, where some homeless people made
Libro feel right at home. Along the way, he was dubious
about the propriety of peeing on unfamiliar-smelling
curbsides and lampposts, but nature triumphed over
company manners. Later, he lay peacefully on the floor

of the bar area while I ate dinner—more concessions to a dog on tour—and then we bedded down. The din of clattering dishes in the hotel's kitchen across the corridor from our room startled both of us awake.

I dressed and went to see the manager to ask if we could please move somewhere quieter. The manager said we occupied the only "dog friendly" room in the hotel. Concessions seemed to go only so far.

One of the things I know about publicity tours, I instructed Libro, is that you can't let glitches bother you. Your attitude has to be that whatever happens is OK. He lifted his head from the pillow, licked my face and closed his eyes. He already knew.

Off we went in the morning, neither of us nervous, one of us covering the rental car's rear window with slobber as we crossed the Golden Gate Bridge. In Berkeley, the Pacifica radio interviewer asked informed questions while Libro, on my lap, snoozed, until he was asked to bark into the microphone, which he did. Because it was California, where people did not sneer at such talk the way they did in New York, I talked a lot about how living with a dog had opened my heart.

"You are probably the first dog to be on the radio," I told him afterward, in the car. He was not impressed, and I had forgotten about Rin Tin Tin.

We lunched with the editor of a magazine about dogs that was as classy as the *New Yorker*. Then we drove to a pet boutique in Marin County, where the same three people who show up at every sparsely attended reading around the country put in an appearance but bought no books. Before our next event, I parked on a quiet, scenic street and fed Libro a dry dinner on the back seat of our rental car.

In downtown San Francisco, we had another reading, this one in a bookstore, with a bigger crowd, including a man who had heard me on the radio that morning and wanted to come home to New York with us. Libro appeared diffident, so I knew the guy was probably not a serial killer. Still, I shuddered. An open heart is a dangerous thing. The stamp of Libro's paw charmed some book buyers and when they asked if it was really *his* paw, I lied.

An old flame, more like a former bonfire, had settled in San Francisco after high-tailing it from New York, pre-Libro. Some years had passed, much ire had diminished and meeting seemed reasonable. I'd told Libro nothing, being curious to observe his gut reaction, which I had come to trust far more than I did my own. We drove over for a visit. The ex-boyfriend, known as Peter Pan, still looked young and handsome and was sweet to Libro, who was generically sweet in response. We trundled off to a magnificent beach, where the males, canine and human, frolicked athletically. The picture postcard birdseye view of the scene—surf, sky, autumn sunshine, man, woman, dog—made me sad. I'm still a sucker for happy family propaganda. How do couples living with dogs ever split up? Luckily, Libro's custody was unshared and I suspect one reason he so mysteriously chose me to live with was that he knew it would be, "just you and me, kiddo," as I'd said somewhere along the way.

At the end of a cordial afternoon, I opened the car's back door for Libro and climbed behind the wheel, telling him we would not move until he sat down. A bit of attention to safety with a dog in the back seat had suddenly occurred to me as a good thing. He obliged.

"So, whaddya think?"

That was me, staring into the rearview mirror before I'd turned the ignition on.

Libro looked back: a look not exactly contemplative, more a reluctant-to-hurt-my-feelings look. Then a snort. And a shrug, which I took to mean either "not much" or, more generously, "nice guy, but I wouldn't want to live with him."

He lay down on the seat. I started the car and pulled away. Neither of us looked back. As Libro once did when I accidentally dropped a can on his head, I shook off the Peter pain I had been carrying for quite a few years. Door closed.

On radio call-in shows and over paw stamping at bookstore signings, I heard stories, saw photographs of

other people's dogs, and smiled accordingly. I had
joined a club, the dog people club. And although we
did not flash our car headlights at each other as members of the Volkswagen-owning club used to do, or
wear secret lapel pins like the CIA club members do,
or certain colors as gang members do, we dog people
recognized one another and felt perhaps a tad superior
to those who were not in our club. Still, in this as in
other groups I had drifted into and out of all my life,
there were some dissonances, some jagged edges, and
some ways in which I did not "fit" the collective iden-
tity of the group.

From the time it became apparent that Libro and I
were going to be together for as long as we both would
live, I had been showered with advice from the dog-
people club. Most of this, I appreciated. I especially appreciated the wise folks who said that Libro should live
my life as opposed to my living his. My life lacked a
backyard or a husband, but it included television lights
and many friends, so that part of the dog people code
suited me and, apparently, suited him. But far too
many folks for my taste referred to theirs and mine
as our "babies." They addressed their canines in a
coochy-coo voice that made me cringe. I always spoke
to Libro as though he was my peer, though I was already getting hints that, young as he was, he might be
smarter, wiser, and more profound than I was. I have
been many things in my lifetime, but Libro's "mommy"

was not among them. To me, he was bodyguard, confidante, resident exterminator, muse, and Saturday night date, not baby.

Actually, the longer we lived together, the more our life took on the quality of a buddy movie. We had the shared busted-out-of-a-straitjacket enthusiasm of Thelma and Louise, the instinct for adventure and the watching-each-other's-back ethics of Butch Cassidy and the Sundance Kid. We balanced each other like Don Quixote and Sancho Panza, although I couldn't tell you which of us was which.

I had, at times, confused him with a doll, but been set straight by wiser heads than mine, including Libro himself. The first weekend he spent in my custody, a baseball cap lying on the sidewalk inspired in me an irresistible urge to accessorize, but he refused to allow it. Irritated, indignant, he shook the cap off. Every time I observed dressed up dogs—two white bulldogs at Halloween, for example, adorned as a top-hatted gentleman and a tutu-clad ballerina—I'd look at Libro, he'd look back, pulling away with "no way" written all over his curled lips and knitted brow.

The best we did in the costuming department was to enter a holiday contest with Libro wearing a small sign around his neck that said, "I am a nudist." We got second place. The window dresser in me envisioned adorning him with a diamond stud in his dark floppy ear, but the folks in the dog run, who quickly became my Greek chorus, commented dourly—"Beware! Beware!"—afraid that other dogs would tear the stud out. Their dogs, presumably. And not in anger but in play.

That day in New York when Libro unaccountably made himself part of my life, I'd had an unspoken secret and a vision. The secret was, "I'll keep you if you pay for yourself," which sounds hard-hearted, but I'd never known a dog before and I was a single woman writer, somewhat phobic about dependents. The vision was, "I see you riding down the Pacific Coast Highway in the back seat of a convertible, wearing Armani sunglasses." Libro *had* paid for himself, standing under the desk or nestling his head in my lap as I wrote the book that got the trip that tested my ability to condense our story into sound bites. Now we were actually driving away from San Francisco and down the Pacific Coast Highway. I'd scotched the convertible idea, fearing storms or rollovers. He'd scotched the sunglasses, along with the other accessories I'd dreamed up.

We rolled into Menlo Park, where the local independent bookstore had gotten the art of selling exactly right—a whole window devoted to us (huge photograph, many books) and a reading to which customers could bring their dogs. As we say in Spanish, "*eso es vivir.*" Now, that's living! And good business, for the store was packed. A woman who rescued greyhounds sat right in the front row with two dogs at her feet.

Libro, who generally growled at high-strung hounds, was on good public behavior. A Bernaise mountain dog flopped in the rear, several shepherds sat politely, some white puffy dogs snuggled on people's laps and a scattering of mutts sprawled all over the floor.

"*Abajo*," I said, and Libro lay down at my feet, looking smugly out at the audience. Showing off his bilingual ability had become part of our road *schtick*. I began to read from the book. Libro snored slightly. I came to the part where I named him "Libro," and he stood up. Maybe he thought I was calling his name to draw him back from dreamland, but it sure as hell looked as though he was taking a bow. The humans giggled, but the dogs began to bark. The greyhounds barked first, then the dogs in the row behind, squeaky barks, squawky barks, basso barks, all the way back to the Bernaise and around the room in a wave.

I panicked, but the wave subsided as soon as Libro, on my instruction, lay down again. So I went on. But every time "Libro" occurred on the page, he stood and the wave started up. I got used to it.

"*Abajo*," I said. The chorus of barks became a murmur and an occasional yelp.

The store sold every copy they had. One customer even followed us to the rental car, where I had a few extras stored in the trunk.

"Attaboy," I said, as we drove off in a cloud of success. "Good dog."

We had a recreational interlude heading south again on the Pacific Coast Highway. My pumpernickel-colored New York City dog raced back and forth and spun in circles on an empty, wide beach, midafternoon on a clear, warming, sunny day and suddenly, in the sky—a bird, a plane, a . . . ? A man with wings. I knew that, but Libro didn't, and as the man drifted downward, then plunked onto the sand, I held the growling canine by his collar and tried to set things right.

"Will you let my dog smell you so he knows you're human?" I called out. Don't people say this sort of thing to one another on California beaches all the time?

The man agreed to be sniffed and he picked up his wings. Libro poked around with his nose and stopped growling. We three walked together, peacefully, up the beach and over a hill, where we came upon the hang-gliding school from which the winged man had begun his journey.

After a quick game of welcoming tug with Libro, the young, trim, tanned man in cutoffs running the school told me that when the humans are in the sky, Icarus-like, the birds play with them. I looked up and sure enough, high above our heads, interspecies games of "dare" and "chicken" were being conducted. For an instant, I actually saw all of nature in tune—ocean, sky, birds, humans and dogs. Try putting that into a sound bite that doesn't end up on the cutting room floor.

Thanksgiving weekend was approaching, and like any traveling show, we were taking time off from performing. Having been assured that Libro was a good visitor, which meant he did not pee on the floor in other people's houses, my old school friend Carolyn had invited us to spend the holiday with her in Santa Cruz. I'd been there several times, including many years before, when Carolyn's cats produced an attack of wheezing that led me to a local motel. Now the coast was clear, the cats gone, and Carolyn a surprisingly dog-friendly person, who spoke to Libro in an adult, educated way.

Her house was a leaky, wooden, rust-colored Victorian, two stories tall, with a high pitched roof, fronted by a deep colonnaded porch. Carolyn put us in a second-floor bedroom unheated but for a plug-in radiator and many layers of quilts. Libro and I snuggled through the chilly night. He was on top of the layers and I was below them, enduring his snores, shuffles, and jangling metal tags so irritating at home but so comforting on the road.

The next day, we three visited a dog beach called Dog Beach, below the lighthouse on West Cliff Drive, where the different slant of light falling on the Pacific Ocean and the large number of dogs who made California their home elicited nary a flicker from Libro's flopping ears or alert eyes as being either strange or daunting. Avoiding the crashing ocean waves and the other dogs, he raced in the sand solo, managing to keep me within visual range (as I did him) as he circled and spun yet again. Don't get too used to this, I was thinking, we don't have too much sand on the island of Manhattan. And it's winter in New York, too.

By turkey time that afternoon, Libro, not being on the invitation list, had to stay behind alone in that big house, finding his spot on a velvet-upholstered window seat, looking very much like a late-nineteenth-century children's book illustration. He watched with longing as Carolyn and I drove off to the home of her nearby friends. But gluttony among strangers soon left me eager to leave and check on "the boy." Carolyn, enjoying herself, sent me ahead on foot with her house keys in hand.

Up the darkened porch I went after a brisk walk, to the front door of the house, where only one light had been left burning. I put the key in the lock, ears pricked for the sound of canine nails clattering toward the door. But the key would not turn.

I heard Libro breathing on the other side of the door. I shifted to other keys on the ring, but to no avail. Libro's breathing was steady, not panicky, as I stepped back to reconnoiter. Ah, there was another door at the back of the house, up a few concrete steps, leading to the kitchen.

I skirted the darkened house, accompanied by a tattoo of canine nails. By the dim outside lamp, through the glass panes of the kitchen door, I saw Libro sitting expectantly on the shiny floor, as though

I might toss him a biscuit from the great outdoors. I inserted one key, then another, only to be stymied again. I tapped on the pane, pressed my lips to the glass, which caused Libro to stand on his hind legs, a posture that caused him pain.

"Get down," I said and returned to the front of the house.

He followed. *Click click*.

Back and forth I went, from porch to kitchen, accompanied by *click* and *click*. Kitchen to porch. *Clickety click*.

Defeated and on the verge of tears, I sat down on the porch in front of the door, eye level with a brass mailbox slot. I lifted the flap.

There were Libro's amber eyes open wide, playful. Who had invented this game?

A reddish pink tongue that I knew to be quite long tried wiggling its way through the slot, toward me.

"Careful baby, you'll get splinters!"

He did not withdraw.

There I sat, explaining the situation, the mystery of why the keys did not work, while a stumpy tail I could not see surely wagged, for what seemed like hours but was not even one, talkin' the night away 'til my friend Carolyn came home and laughed.

In Carmel, "dog friendly" was an understatement. An entire crescent of beachfront was set aside for canine play. At the red tile–roofed, white stucco hotel over-looking the beach, partly owned by Doris Day, life-time crusader for animal rights, canine guests got their own menus, bowls, and beds. Libro and I set up in the vast living room, in front of a wall-to-wall flagstone fireplace. Locals, drawn by a story in the newspaper, trickled in with their dogs. Hotel guests arrived. The four-legged guests climbed onto the chintz furniture and settled down, while their well-dressed human companions took to the floor. Libro remained in posi-tion this time, lying quietly at my feet. While I was signing and stamping books afterward, I chitchatted, as one does.

"Do you have a dog?" I asked a thin elderly man on arm crutches, with a hearing aid in each ear. He had arrived unaccompanied.

"No," he said, "but I'm in love with a dog," and pro-ceeded to tell me about the black Lab next door who came to visit him every day. Tears formed at the edges of his eyes.

In the pre-Libro days, this was exactly the kind of blather that made me roll my eyes, if not think of call-ing the psych medics. Now I merely touched the man's arm sympathetically and added some slurpy kisses to the inscription in his book. I knew then that I was ruined.

All along, I checked Libro for signs of burnout. There were none. Each time he jumped into a rental car as eagerly as the first time. He entered every radio station, hotel or bookstore tail up, ears flapping, nose on overdrive, as though something magnificent awaited him. If there were three people in the audience or a hundred, a crowded studio or a setup with one camera in a hotel room—as long as there was attention, plus water, biscuits and me, he was happy. He never met a fan he didn't like.

We went home after Carmel, Libro traveling in his little house without fuss or medication and arriving in New York without incident. He slid onto his own cushy bed and appeared to clutch it for dear life— home, home!—and then he slept for half a day.

There were more East Coast promotions, including a television show in Nassau County which we almost missed because of ice on the roads. The host asked me a lot of nervy questions about my sex life as a single woman. He also warned me not to let Libro turn his back to the camera, which would, given that he had a stump of a tail, allow the audience a view of a part of him better left unseen.

Our curtain call was a bookstore signing in a snowy upstate New York town, where the store's owners had "lost" their boxer and wanted to play with Libro much more than they wanted to promote books. We had a slight accident on a slip of icy road returning home, caused by the car behind us, which left Libro understandably wary about riding in the back seat again. Just as well that we were ready to retire.

In the dead of the winter, when days were short and lonely, when it was just Libro and me and new words falling slowly onto a new page, without a spotlight or applause, I would look deep into those amber eyes and say, as Bogie does to Bergman in *Casablanca*, "Hey kiddo, we'll always have California."

# 3

# City Slicker

> . . . the city, where the air trembled like a
> tuning-fork with unimaginable possibilities.
> —Willa Cather

B ut the cheering always dies down and the spotlight always fades in show business. We were en-
sconced again in the brownstone on Manhattan's
Upper West Side, in the joys and perils of city life,
streets covered with snow, ice, and salt and in Libro's
ongoing conversion of freewheeling Auntie Mame
into apron-clad Betty Crocker.

"*Bienvendo, Libro,*" Eddie the mailman said the first
morning after our trip that they met. Welcome back.
"*¿Donde estabas? ¿En un avion? ¿En television?*" He was

treating Libro like a rock star, inquiring, while he pushed his cart down the street, what cities he had been to, what television shows he had been on.

"Welcome home, Libro," said the doorman at the corner building, removing his gloves and reaching into his pocket for a treat.

"Big D," the UPS driver, was in his double-parked delivery truck toward the end of the street, warming himself before facing the next load of holiday packages he would have to distribute. Libro stopped walking and wagged his tail, though he dared not sit down on the snowy sidewalk. "Big D" opened the truck door and Libro jumped in. At other times, in fairer weather, while the door was open and the driver unloaded boxes onto his handtruck in the rear, Libro liked to sit up high on the seat behind the steering wheel. The UPS shade of brown exactly matched Libro's coat. I had considered investigating animal modeling agencies, to see if he could be used in a UPS ad campaign. Now, as a thin sleet began to fall outside, Big D took him on his lap, removing his gloves to rub Libro's ears, and the better part of me decided that I'd been stage mother enough for a while.

Walking carefully into a biting wind with Libro, trying to avoid mountains of ice-melting, paw-burning salt that supers had inconsiderately heaped along the sidewalk, we caught up on the neighborhood's goings on. While we'd been enjoying California sunshine, Lola, a remote vizsla who played Beatrice to Libro's forever yearning Dante, had acquired a younger "brother." We met them on the corner. The puppy showed his teeth as Libro approached. Lola kept her nose in the air while her new sibling snarled, letting us all know that he would like to eat Libro for breakfast.

Rick, the man these vizslas lived with, was a special friend of Libro's, having kept him overnight while I went out of town for a speaking engagement. It had been our first separation. My dog had never been to doggy daycare because I was always home. I'd never left town because he was always home. But good-natured Libro had turned out to be an anxious, ill-behaved overnight guest.

When Rick retired for the night, closing his bedroom door, Lola went to her fluffy pillow on the living room floor, where Libro was surely welcome, though given her street behavior, it might be a frosty welcome. How torn Libro must have been between the girl of his dreams and his caretaker. In the end, human warmth won out over canine love and Libro "boxed" Rick's bedroom door, begging for entry. When it wasn't forthcoming—everybody had their own preferences about dogs in their beds or even their bedrooms—my confident, self-possessed little prince had scratched away at the closed door in frustration or

panic. My friendship with Rick had suffered a chill after that and Libro was no longer welcome there.

Rick is a strong man and he exerted remarkable physical control over his tough, unneutered, testosterone-
laden, sibling-protective young male dog, while holding
Lola steady on the wintry street corner. Libro barked
and backed away. Catastrophe averted. We had not
turned Riverside Drive into a bloodbath. But Libro, accustomed to being quite generally beloved in the 'hood,
was bewildered by this turn of events. He looked from
the dogs in their matching forest-green fleece coats and
the man in his black down jacket to me, brow crinkled,
with "huh?" written all over his scrunched-up face.

"Jealousy is not a rational emotion," I, the Great Ex-
plainer, said, apparently bewildering him even more.

To repair his self-esteem, we walked to Broadway,
the chilling wind slicing across the Hudson River and
whipping us forward. In the Korean grocery store, Libro did something that sounded like "anja"—he sat,
in the Korean language, as the grocer told him to. I
wondered how many languages he was capable of
learning. The grocer beamed, as he always did, and I
applauded. Nobody snarled. I bought several bunches
of red tulips. Sometimes repair is easy; often not.

Some days later, when the temperature reached
above freezing and the streets ran with slush, we visited the dog run. It was not very crowded. Many
people, I'd discovered, simply walked their dogs for toi-

let breaks year-round, but especially in winter. Apparently they—or their dogs—didn't crave society the way Libro and I did. Or exercise, though I was beginning to hear talk of indoor gyms for canines and swimming pools, too, which would be good therapy for Libro's stiff leg if only he didn't hate the water. A few folks in the run—but not their dogs—shunned us at first, feeling that they, too, could have written books about *their* remarkable canines. This, I told Libro, was the price of celebrity. They would get over it. Or they would not. We stuck to old friends who had grown up with Libro, members all, I liked to say, of the class of '97: Sophie and Mattie, Portuguese Water Dogs, Ella and Sampson, rottweilers who made Libro look like a midget as we walked together from the run, past the bare trees, hurrying home to warm apartments.

Soon we were deeply grooved in connubial routine. I drank coffee. Libro ate breakfast. Because his tummy was as turbulent as my grandma's had been—digestive problems run in the family—various soothing powders were sprinkled over his food. Then came the morning medication ritual: one pill for him, one for me. This was beginning to take longer than it had before because we were putting more pills into our respective mouths.

He got smelly fish oil capsules to keep his skin from itchy dryness. His right hind leg required the most attention. Though he walked and ran as well as any dog, even climbed four flights of stairs easily, mostly using his muscular chest, shoulders and forelegs, Libro was somewhat out of alignment. He slightly favored his left leg, which moved without friction, but the increasing stiffness of his right leg had spread to his hips. All his joints were a tad creaky. For this, Libro took three large green capsules, laden with shark cartilage and other good things for joints.

I, being a great deal older than Libro, even counting each dog year as equivalent to seven human years, was becoming a tad creaky myself, so while he swallowed glucosamine and chondroiten, I took calcium supplements. I took vitamin E capsules to protect my own skin from itchy dryness. Depending on the pollen count, I downed an antihistamine. I had drops for my drying eyes. In naivete or recklessness, since I was beyond childbearing age, and in spite of dire warnings that made me feel like Eve chomping into the apple, I was also taking tiny hormone supplements.

If there had been medication to remove the bump that had appeared on my right foot, I would have taken that, too. The bump was a bunion, a hard swelling over the joint behind the big toe, which made my foot look exactly like my grandma's. The only remedy was surgery, which would have kept me from getting around for weeks, including walking or traveling with Libro, so it was clearly out of the question. Besides, the word "surgery" made me nauseous. So I was left with an old lady bunion and the despair of looking over my spring wardrobe and putting aside the collection of sexy sandals.

While the four flights of stairs presented no problem for Libro, they did for me. I had to be organized. Forgetting anything meant extra trips up and down. Though I had lived this way for more than a decade before Libro arrived, his presence made organization more urgent because there were more things to collect before leaving the apartment. Keys. Leash. Poop bags. A sweater or a coat. The dog. Plus anything I would need for a morning errand—trash to throw out, letters to mail, cash for a newspaper, or more cash for dog food if that morning's breakfast had emptied the supply.

I didn't always organize perfectly, which was fine when I was single, but not so fine with a pair of amber eyes at the level of my knees taking it all in. Not to mention that he had to follow me out the door, stop, one foot on the top stair, while I searched my pockets, follow me back inside to collect what I had forgotten. By now, he knew the routine, and if I stopped on the stairs and spun around on my heels, I could swear he sighed, an indulgent sigh. I didn't mind being a flibbergibbet, but I did mind having a witness.

Having attended to our combined well being, we descended to the street, our playground, theater and village green. The street was a communal gathering place like the old village green for Libro even more than it was for me, since I could make use of modern conveniences like telephones and e-mail to keep up with the world. For him, the street was corner news-stand, cell phone, fax, e-mail, discussion list, and blog. He would not only see friends and enemies of the canine variety, but catch up on recent happenings through his nose, his primary investigative tool. To say Libro "sniffed" minimizes the infinite variety of ways in which he took in information from what he could inhale along the sidewalks, under the trees, or beneath the tires of parked cars, not to mention the expansive tableau that was Riverside Park. His nose told him who had passed by, how long ago, what sex they were, and a lot of other things I could not translate, but could observe. He could sniff contemplatively, as though he had to think the information over, or intensely, as though he was studying a difficult portion of the Talmud. He could, nose down, register alarm or anger, surprise, bemusement, or dissent. And he could leave messages of his own that would provoke other canines to similar reactions. He was a great message-leaver.

Likewise, Libro's barks registered his response to street life. He was not a frequent barker. When I was new to dogs and he was terrified and traumatized, he had been so quiet that I'd asked the vet if his vocal cords were healthy. But his lungs turned out to be fine and strong, and he exercised them in public far more than he did in the privacy of our home. For a sweet-looking dog, he had a ferocious "get out of here" rumbling, basso bark that came from deep within his large chest, usually directed at a large Irish wolfhound who lived in a building a few doors away and whose owner raced away with the jittery dog whenever Libro was on the street.

Because his smelling ability was as hyperdeveloped as any canine's, Libro barked at things I couldn't see. I decided, after a while, that he was not hallucinating, just smelling an Irish wolfhound miles across the Hudson, walking a New Jersey pathway. Or a rat scampering into a hole in the park. He had a yippier, "pay attention to me" bark that usually emerged when we met another person with a dog if both that person and I lavished too much attention on the other dog. I thought of this as his "only child" bark. While many dogs make barking sounds during playful tussles, Libro rarely did. He took recreation seriously, and at times, with his intense eyes focused and concentrating, he seemed to be playing chess rather than frolicking.

By spring, doctor's visits had become a fixture in our weekly schedule because acupuncture turned out to be helpful for what was now being called arthritis in his legs and hips. Libro loved his doctor and all the people who worked with him, unlike other dogs I'd seen cower or whimper and try to escape as they were dragged into the vet's office. Libro went eagerly. The old behavior of jumping up on people and things made a resurgence, in spite of the pain, when he reached the door, so eager was he to enter. Sometimes he pulled me down West End Avenue toward the office even when we had no scheduled appointment. I said that if he wasn't careful, he would turn into a hypochondriac, as many other people in my human family already were. The treats stuffed into his mouth on arrival and departure were just part of the attraction. I believe he knew that he would find help and care there and that he always felt better when he left.

We had a routine at the doctor's, too. An assistant lowered the steel examining table nearly to the floor and Libro got on. Then it was raised to about my waist height, Libro looking slightly dubiously over the side as it moved. I climbed aboard, sat and held Libro across my lap. When the doctor came with his needles, Libro thrust his right haunch in the air, offering both hip and thigh. In went the needles. Out of the room went the doc, lowering the lights. For half an hour, Libro lay still, like a mountain range with TV antennae stuck all over it, while I told him a story: "Once upon a time, there was a little brown dog lost in the park and along came a woman who . . ." Or I sang: "You'll Never Walk Alone" and "This Little Light of Mine." Unlike the good singers at school graduation ceremonies who winced when I tried to make melodies or unceremoniously shushed me, Libro just closed his eyes and flicked his tail.

*This* was the woman who lived during her college years on scotch, chocolate ice cream, and steak because thinking of what to eat each day was too great a distraction from the Great Thoughts that crowded her mind? Who once coolly kissed her date goodnight at the door, then secretly rushed off to meet his older brother for a nightcap?

Our life together continued to expand. When a large black standard poodle named Rocky moved to New York from Houston with Janet the museum curator and Ed the poet that summer, we had new companions. Rocky was only two years old, and he had a propensity for humping other dogs. I'd long ago learned that this was not sexual behavior and therefore not gender-defined, so when he tried to mount Libro one afternoon while Janet and I were sitting on a park bench with our dogs, with the thump of tennis balls from the city courts as background, I shrugged. Libro was facing me, eyes widened: "What's going on back there?" Janet pulled Rocky off.

Whatever was going on stopped, but the instrument of the event, to put it as delicately as possible, was still with us. Rocky had an enormous bright-red erection. Obviously, it hurt. He whined. Libro looked bewildered and I watched him check what I believed to be his natural impulse to approach those in pain. He took a step forward, retreated, and sat down. Janet and I, sad to say, giggled. Rocky winced and whined some more and walked in a circle, bowlegged.

"What should we do?"

Janet and I could hardly speak.

"I don't know. What should we do?"

"What would we do if it were human?"

Now, the subject of the dog's genitals is not discussed in polite society, even among the most experienced dog people of my acquaintance. There is a tinge of the prurient about mentioning it, even noticing it, which pretty much served to silence me when I was perplexed about why Libro, the first canine I had known, would get excited at peculiar times or exhibit other behaviors equally incomprehensible to me, separated as I was from him by the gulf between our species and our genders. Male dog people on the whole were downright blubbery and berserk on the question of neutering their animals. Only one such person ever gave me an answer to my questions: "Human ones are irrational, too," he said. I stopped asking.

So as Rocky the poodle winced and whined, Janet and I were so absolutely floored by the problem, which refused to go away, that we became hysterical. What would we do if it were human?

We decided to pour water on it.

Just as we were pulling Rocky on his leash toward the nearest water fountain, a jogger came by. A male jogger. And oh, if looks could kill.

Libro had one incorrigible flaw when it came to street behavior. He, who rarely made a fuss about anything, barked furiously at anyone going through the garbage—the large green plastic cans set in front of our building like sentinels or even those oversized wastebaskets on street corners. People did this all the time, even though Mayor Giuliani was leading a "crackdown" on "quality of life" offenses. Black or white or brown or blended, young or old or in between, male or female, junkies, drunks or the merely impoverished—it didn't matter. Libro went wild if they scavenged or treasure hunted in the garbage, even if they only approached the cans and were about to touch them. I explained that some people couldn't buy their own newspapers or even food, but no amount of Marxist theorizing could dissuade him or even shut him up.

Many of these were the same people who slept at night on benches along Riverside Drive or in the park itself. And Libro knew them. "The Cat Lady," always begging for coins on Broadway, used at least some of those coins to buy food for the feral strays that lived in dens under the stone park walls. The rest, I presume from her behavior, went for rotgut whiskey. The

"Book Guy" and "the Baseball-cap Guy" had crack pipes in their pockets. All knew Libro's name, all played with him. It didn't matter. None of these citizens of the nether side of the city were allowed, in Libro's great scheme of things, to touch the garbage.

Nearly all the dogs I knew who had been rescued from abusive homes or abandoned on city streets or plucked from animal shelters had idiosyncrasies. Many flinched if anyone raised a hand, even to put a hat on their heads or brush their own hair. One dog fled at the sound and smell of a beer can being opened. Another barked at men in Hasidic garb. Quite a few had marked gender preferences or avoidances. My only clues to Libro's history were his affection for black men, his attitude toward cats, and that behavior around the garbage cans.

Rooting in the trash appeared to violate his code of civilized behavior—such was the indignation with which he barked at those who dared to commit such transgression. I also thought it possible that the garbage cans had held dinner during however much time he had spent abandoned and roaming around. Could he be protecting himself against the possibility of future trauma—was his behavior a form of insurance?—by becoming guardian of the neighborhood trash? Who knew? I did know that I could never teach Libro to walk on by under those conditions. I knew, also, that the neighborhood street people learned that when Libro approached, they should immediately step away from the cans and smile at him. And they did.

Libro was now so familiar with the routines of his life that he knew a certain yellow plastic bag came from the pet store, that Deborah the lawyer who lived with Barclay the mutt always had treats in her waist pouch that she was willing to share, and that though I might leave him alone for a few hours, I would always return and welcome enthusiastic greetings. He knew that puppies were not quite responsible for their flailing attempts to control their own bodies and play with him. And he knew what a baby was.

We were in Riverside Park, out for a stroll close to sunset. Sometimes, at this time of day, I liked to walk with Libro along the rocks down near the Hudson River, stopping to sit on the flatter stones to watch the sky turn pink and the sun begin to disappear behind the taller buildings on the New Jersey side. In fact, summer sunset was a neighborhood ritual time, when people with or without dogs often came out to sprawl on the benches along Riverside Drive, their eyes fixed on the same display of sinking sun over still water, as though they were all at the movies.

But Libro and I were down in the park, walking along. We passed a large, musical, extended-family picnic with lots of Spanish being spoken and sung. A baby crawled on the grass, away from the party. Libro liked babies and had some experience with them because our neighborhood was replete with infants, usually dangling from people's bodies in snuglis. He was very attracted. If permitted, he would approach and sniff the baby's feet, sometimes, licking them, which humans referred to as "kissing." In this as in so many other things, trying to understand why Libro did what he did expanded my knowledge of certain arcane subjects—like babies' feet or babies' bodies, which, any parent will tell you, do smell different from yours and mine. They have, I learned, more lactose. Sweet-smelling.

So sniffing babies' feet while they safely dangled from grown-ups might be all right, but that day in the park, deciding to go visit a crawling infant was not. Especially when I could see two men in the crowd of fiesta-makers eye the dog, then the baby. To their eyes, he was about to charge. They started to move toward him.

"*Libro! No! Siéntate, Libro.*" I shouted.

And he did, dead in his tracks, far from the baby, stop and sit.

Thereafter, Libro sat for babies everywhere. He sat on the side streets, the avenues, the park drive, when a carriage or a stroller came by or yet another snugli. He sat until he was invited to engage. If not, he looked disappointed but did not insist. Until one day, a toddler came stumbling and bumbling along the street like a drunk, his hand clenched by a parent. Libro did not sit.

"Libro, there's a baby. What do you do when you see a baby?"

He looked at the parent, looked at me, up and down the street, straight through the toddler. They passed us by while I held Libro's leash. He hadn't sat. And then I realized that the small creature walking was not, in Libro's mind, a baby. Babies don't walk. The authors of dog-training books had neglected to alert me that in order to teach my dog to behave, I had to be sure to define my terms. "Baby," for example.

∽

Although experts say that domesticated dogs learn to cohabitate with the human race by becoming Ph.D.s in the body language of people, I would say that after four years of living together, I had become adept at reading Libro's. Boxers' eyes are set more closely together than those of other breeds, hampering peripheral vision, but giving them what can easily be taken (or mis-taken) for human facial configurations. I read the infinite variety of Libro's expressions like a shelf full of cheap novels.

A rather polite expression, something like a well-brought-up preppy kid came over him near the biscuit bin in the pet food store, which was placed seductively low near the checkout counter and therefore unavoidable if you took your dog shopping, as I always did.

"Please, *please* can I have that?" involved sitting without being told to and looking up with pleading eyes.

He had the same look sitting at my feet as I unloaded groceries, heedless of whether the objects I drew from the plastic bags were popcorn, chocolate, or steak. And I thought canines' olfactory equipment made for swell discriminators. A variation on polite pleading was over-the-top manipulative and a mark, from the very beginning, of what a showman, clown, or ham he was: "I've been starving for months and only you can save me from certain death by feeding me that." This expression was accompanied by the stage business of nearly convincing pathos in his eyes and a sucked-in hollowing of his cheeks, exactly the kind of thing I used to do in high school when I wanted more prominent cheekbones.

"Get away from here or I will kill you" appeared as a ferocious frown when an enemy, like the lanky Irish wolfhound or the unneutered brown bulldog residing many streets away walked within two blocks of Libro. Sometimes in the midst of such menacing, Libro would turn to me with a tail wag and something like a wink, which I read as "Don't worry, little lady, I'll take care of this varmit."

Once, when a bird flew through an open window into the apartment, he was not Sir Galahad, but a fiery, brimstoned witch hunter from old Salem, stalking the bewildered bird around the living room, barking ferociously and then trying to leap to the top of the floor-to-ceiling bookshelves, where the bird cowered. The dog's expression that day, I can only translate as: "*De debbil* has appeared." The bird was terrified and only managed to escape the way it had come when I removed Libro from the room, allowing peace and sanity to prevail.

"Yum/sigh," was an expression accompanied by slowly closing eyelids as he tucked himself into my armpit while I lay reading on the couch. Over the years of living with me, Libro was exposed to a wide range of literature, from pulpy detective novels in which the female sleuth always got her man (although not in the traditional way) to the hilarity of David Sedaris, which made me giggle, nearly upsetting Libro's comfort, to occasional rereadings of favorites by Brontë or Woolf, which I did with such concentration that Libro nudged me and licked my face to see if I remembered he was there. Weightier tomes of American history and biography, usually those exposing the lies of the past or the dark sides of people's lives, often made me sigh. Sometimes he sighed, too, and sometimes he sniffed the volume in my hands. I could find no coherent taste in his reactions.

Eyes huge. Brow knit. Head slightly cocked. Looking at me. This was my favorite facial expression: "What is that?"

"What is that?" he seemed to say one afternoon as an aging Chesapeake Bay retriever rolled down the street with her back legs supported by what I would describe as training wheels. He had seen many people using apparatus of many kinds to navigate the sidewalks. Anyone with a walker or in a wheelchair aroused his sympathy, and I'd had to restrain him from rushing over to walk beside them. On various occasions, we had volunteered together to feed homeless people at holiday times and then, when he wasn't distracted by the turkey and cranberry and pumpkin pie, he had been perfectly calm around, if not disinterested in, crutches, canes, scooters, and wheelchairs.

He was fascinated and apparently confused by Lama, the female coppery dog-on-wheels, who lived with Olga, a Peruvian anthropologist on the first floor of our building, confused or worried him. I told him that the dog's hind legs had lost their strength but that she was not in pain. He needn't worry because he was a strong boy in spite of his own gimpy leg and surely he would never need such an apparatus. Libro used his nose to investigate the wheels very carefully while Lama stood by patiently and, it seemed to me, sadly resigned, not to her young male inquisitor, but to her wheely fate. Afterward, Olga remarked in *español* that his attitude was "*sensible*" and Libro was "*un caballero*," sensitive and gentlemanly.

"What is that?" he asked on the lawn at the cathedral of St. John the Divine, where I took Libro for the Blessing of the Animals ceremony. Goats, llamas, cats,

dogs, and gerbils were all equal in the eyes of the Lord
and invited to receive benedictions. Libro had blessed
the female priest, jumping up to put his paws on her
shoulders as she bent toward him and depositing endless slobbery grateful kisses—his version, I suppose, of
benediction—all over her face. As we walked away,
we came upon a peacock strutting on the cathedral
grounds. Yes, Virginia, there are peacocks in Manhattan. Libro stopped dead and stared as the feathery
thing waddled across the path. I stopped, too. The peacock stopped. And then . . .

And then . . .

Like a visual trumpet blare, an unfolding of irides-
cent blues and greens, the peacock spread its tail. *Ta-
da* and *voila*! Even *my* heart skipped a beat. Libro
turned to stone, jaw dropped, eyes huge. *Étonné* is the
word in French, meaning stunned, turned to stone.
Plain, simple awe was what he showed, not prompted
to attack or even to bark, just to sit there gaping until
the extravaganza waddled away.

Later, along Riverside Drive strode a vision in black,
a nun in full habit with a large crucifix bouncing on
and off her chest. She looked at Libro and smiled. He
looked back and did the same. Her smile broadened
and I said, "Makes you believe in God, doesn't it?"
I think I meant to say, "Makes you believe in perfection." I regarded Libro's physical beauty and inner

grace as something marvelous, created by a force beyond my understanding, a force different from what made the space shuttle or a French-cut bias skirt. As a gardener, I might have said "nature." As a purportedly rational being of some skepticism, I might have said nothing at all. But I said "God," which endeared me to the nun, who would soon become the less generic Sister Veronica and take her place in Libro's entourage as what I referred to as his spiritual advisor.

Others before me had used similar vocabulary, usually less self-consciously than I did. Virginia Woolf, for example, described her spaniel puppy as "an angel of light" and revealed how her husband Leonard "says seriously she makes him believe in God . . . and this after she has wetted his floor eight times in one day."

Aside from the desire to not be interrupted at work, my domestic attitude toward living with a dog, as it was evolving, was not quite laissez-faire, but close. I didn't keep Libro off the furniture because *mi casa* was *su casa* and besides, I liked having him on the furniture. The bed was off limits because his habits annoyed me—I know long-married couples who face the same problem. I gave him enough treats and toys to keep him happy, but did not discourage others from heaping gifts upon him, even if the gifts proved problematic for me. He got rawhide bones and smelly pig's ears, shampoos and conditioners, collapsible food and water bowls for his travels. A genuine Christmas stocking decorated with white, plastic doggy bones to hang for St. Nick. And toys, lots of toys. Stuffed objects that squeaked and drove me crazy until he tore them apart and I felt justified removing the squeakers. Balls to carry around in his mouth and lose under the furniture until I retrieved them. Things made of rubber or rope to pull on if I was willing to wrench my shoulder muscles.

As Libro was expected to learn and accommodate my preferences, I thought it only fair that, to some measure, I reciprocate. His rules, ideas, and opinions about how our home should be, how the street should be and what was or was not acceptable in the wider world were hardly irrational. They were usually far more orderly than my own.

The toys were always scattered about—the ratty white teddy on the couch, pull toys in different corners—and when I straightened up one afternoon, tossing the toys into their basket, pulling the vacuum cleaner from the closet, Libro watched carefully and then went to sit at the door, waiting for the company that must be coming if I was cleaning. He had a logic of his own.

Nobody came. I dusted the bookshelves. Still nobody came and still he sat waiting at the door. When

I sat down to read in the newly cleaned place, Lord Libro gave up on the door, went to his toy basket in a corner of the kitchen and one by one, removed each toy. The ratty white bear was carried in his mouth, back to the couch. The rope tug-toy returned to the spot under the window. The green rubber ring went to the hallway. On each trip, he looked back at me: This is how I like it. Exactly like this. Explanatory. Defiant.

੦੭

My dear old widowed dad in Florida had interrupted my happy domestic life by asking me to visit. Life where he lived had been turbulent before, during and throughout the long aftermath of November's national elections, when the presidential choice of the Sunshine State had morphed from Al Gore to George Bush, Joe Lieberman to Dick Cheney. While the machinations of state and nation unnerved all its citizens, my father and his cronies in the retirement villages of Dade and Broward counties had taken it all quite personally, having worked to elect the first Jewish vice-president in history. Many of them were angry. My father had a mild heart attack.

Since the election, I had been worried about my father and, while not nearly as ethnically passionate as he, certainly politically stunned. Libro, being a dog, hardly cared who held national office, but he had also been shanghaied into participating in politics. He made an irresistible prop as I worked the subway stations in the neighborhood for a favorite senatorial candidate. Nudist that he was, he had tolerated a campaign button pinned on his collar. Show off that he was, he'd helped entice voters to stop as they emerged from underground.

"What a beautiful dog," they'd say.

"Would you like some campaign literature?" I'd reply.

"What's his name?"

"It's really important that you vote in this election," I'd insist and, if appropriate, I'd lean down and ask Libro to "*da le un beso.*" Citizens who obliged by allowing Libro to lick their faces or their hands were already, I would have bet, on our side.

"*El perro habla español?*"

"Yes, the dog speaks Spanish. Please take some campaign literature."

My father's request for a visit seemed a good opportunity to introduce Libro to tropical climes and to my father, but no, dad huffed, "No dogs allowed in the condo."

"He's probably the only grandson you'll ever have," I answered, sassy daughter that I am, mindful that pretending to be Libro's mommy might be a useful ploy. It didn't work. My father was not only a stickler for rules, but having lived quite alone for six years since my mother's death, rather possessive of me. I would need to go to Florida by myself, leaving Libro.

Leave him where? Mindful of the chewed-up door, I couldn't ask Rick again. Nor did boarding him seem a good idea. I imagined that a once-abandoned fellow would not be happy to be thrust into strange surroundings with people he did not know. Plus, kennel cough. Plus, the expense. If it were me, I'd rather stay where my bed, toys, and food bowl were.

Libro's bed, toys, and food bowl were not only in my apartment, but in my building. He lived not only with me, but with all my neighbors. And he was entirely comfortable with them because, like me, he knew that it takes a building to raise a dog.

During a noisy rainstorm the previous spring, while other dogs around town cowered under beds at each thunderclap and lightning flash, Libro had discovered my carelessness about closing the door that kept him home. He managed to pry it open. I only knew what had transpired when I returned, rain soaked, from errands in the world to a dogless apartment.

But there was a note.

"Libro is with us," Maria had written. As, indeed, he was, in the third-floor apartment warm, dry and in the good company of Maria and Fred. He had actually eased his way into the hallway and wandered around the building until he knocked at Maria's door. I wondered how many other doors he had tried.

So I negotiated four days of care among all the residents of my building while I was in Florida. The opera singer on the fifth floor took charge.

I wrote out these instructions:

- Don't sleep with him. He snores and farts.
- Four things make him happy: food, a walk, a massage, and a hug. He'll show you which one he wants.
- Be wary in the street. Because of his coloring, some people think he's a pit bull and gulp or freeze or head for the hills when they see him. This insults him, but is basically good for you.
- He has three canine enemies: an Irish wolfhound, an overcoiffed black poodle, and a tough rottweiler with testicles. Avoid them at all costs.
- He loves police—because they rescued him— and all male people except those lugging garbage bags full of clanking cans retrieved from trash baskets. He might be looking for a man for me.

I thought I would feel bereft when I left, but I felt free. I didn't have to be home at precisely 5 P.M. for dinner. I could stay out until sunrise. I could go for a stroll and follow my fancy, into a department store if I so desired, or into a movie theatre or on the heels of some southern hunk. I could, if I wished, be a bad woman again. By the time the plane landed in Florida, I was thinking "*eso es vivir,*" oh, this is really living, and considering a quick dash to the Bahamas for an orgy of gambling.

My waiting dad, looking much older, quite pale and a little frail, offered gallantly to carry my small suitcase. I let him. We went out into the humid air, found the car, turned the air conditioning on high and drove to the condo in what I will forever call his Merry Oldsmobile.

"You talk about nothing but that dog," he said at the end of our first day. And so I had. How smart Libro was. How bilingual. How beautiful. How comic. I missed the rhythm of our steps in tandem and the constant communication between us. In Florida, most of the time, I had nobody to talk to. My father went to bed early and was given to long silences at other times.

After the Early Bird Special at a Miami restaurant, and before the third movie my father and I would see together, I called New York. I got the opera singer's answering machine. "You don't have to call me back," I said, "unless there's a problem." But I kind of wished she would.

One of the pleasures of living with Libro was never having to come back to an empty apartment again. When I opened my door at home, he wagged not only his tail, but all the parts of him aft of his chest. The opera singer had overseen a ragtag schedule in which Libro had heard great jazz on the saxophone played by the guy on the first floor, engaged in long talks with the stockbroker on the second, sniffed the lasagna bubbling on the third floor, offered his leash to strange men in the street for a game of tug. He'd been massaged, sung to, hugged, which was a lot more than I had enjoyed.

The man the opera singer was dating had pitched in, even agreeing to walk Libro and obey the rules for removing the dog's excreta from sidewalks, which he'd been queasy about. This impressed the opera singer. Having decided that his willingness to engage life's messier side augured well for his future as a member of the diaper-changing brigade, her doubts about marrying him dissipated and an engagement ring now sparkled on her finger. The only glitch, she told me, was that every once in a while, Libro sat down wherever he was, looked out the window, and whimpered. I knew how he felt.

ᐩ

Living in Manhattan is a constant lesson in the inevitability of change. In my neighborhood, a supermarket might become the ground floor of a luxury apartment building virtually overnight. A movie theater would become a supermarket. Within the buildings, people moved in for a year and pushed on, marrying and needing a nursery room or giving up on city life and heading for the wilderness or having built their careers halfway, leaving for parts of the west where they would become presidents of corporations. Some of the dogs Libro and I had come to know on the streets and in the dog run had disappeared when spring came each year and some people did, too, so it was impossible to know whether a moving van or the Grim Reaper had come for them. The saxophone player went to Los Angeles, the opera singer married her boyfriend and moved with him to a larger, fancier apartment in midtown. A vizsla and a young married couple I barely saw moved into that apartment for a while, but the dog never left the apartment. I always wondered what they did about her waste. And Lama died.

All I knew was that Olga's face was streaked with tears as she described "putting Lama to sleep." We were not then as close as we would become, so I did not hear in detail about the sad last months of Lama's life, her incontinence, and the beginning of pain, but I could see Olga's pain and quickly put that possibility for myself out of my mind. Libro was immortal. Plus, he was still young and strong.

Over the weeks that followed, I lent Libro to Olga every once in a while, as compensation for her doglessness and a way of keeping up his language skills.

"*Siéntate*," she would say. He sat.

"*Dáme un beso*," she said. He kissed her.

On a few occasions, when I gave talks at colleges and could not avoid being away overnight, Libro stayed with Olga. Close to 5 P.M., his dinnertime, he would go to her apartment door and indicate plainly that he wanted to go upstairs, to his home. At first, being as empathetic a dog person as I am, Olga did not want to return him to an empty apartment, but Libro was insistent, so she did. He liked his own dish, as do I. And he wanted to sleep in his own bed. Amen to that.

The changes continued. Ben and Emily, fresh from Cambridge, Massachusetts, moved into a second-floor apartment after the stockbroker who lived there gave up on our bohemian, left-leaning neighborhood to join his fellow Republicans on the East Side. The day the young couple arrived with all their worldly goods, Libro pushed his way past the slightly ajar door to inspect the apartment or to search for its former tenant. He had as much trouble with change as I did, maybe more. But he dashed toward Ben, a writer and former college wrestler, whom he'd never seen before and who, unlike so many of Libro's passions, was a white man. Ben applied considerable muscle strength tussling with Libro, who appeared to love every minute. Libro treated Emily, who was studying for a doctorate in psychology, more gently, not because she was about my size, but because he was nothing less than a courtier when it came to women.

Not long afterward, Ben and Emily adopted a large brown mixed breed named Kaya, who had one green eye and one blue one. Kaya, too, was a rescued dog. We didn't seem to go in for breeders and pedigrees in my neighborhood. Unlike Libro, who became a member of my household by "accident"—though I was beginning to wonder about that—Kaya was chosen. Ben and Emily had studied websites for months before moving to New York and they had their eyes on Kaya for some time. That she was still in the shelter waiting for a home when they got there seemed nothing less than a miracle.

Libro retained his position as the Prince of the building. He had been there longer than Kaya and so, by dog logic, it was more his than hers. Also, Kaya was female and he was male, which counted for a lot and not only in dog logic.

෮

My father was a card player, a good one. After he had a stroke, when the doctors announced he'd made a complete recovery, he whispered to me that it wasn't true, that when he dealt a deck, the feeling of his fingers moving on the cards' surface was different. Subtly, but definitively. So it is natural that I think in terms of playing card metaphors: The hand I was holding by then, four years into living with Libro, had all four suits—hearts (friends), diamonds (worldly goods), spades (work) and clubs (entertainment). Lots of face cards, perhaps an excess of Queens, but no Jack.

Although there always had been, still were, and always would be many men in my life, the idea of Prince Charming at this stage seemed like more trouble than it might be worth. Besides, I was already taken. I had a Significant Other and though it might seem odd to some, since he walked on four legs and barked, Libro blotted out any would-be competitors. I had even asked my lawyer to revise my will, making sure Libro was provided for—not by some kooky bequest of all my lands and riches, as I'd heard of some rich eccentrics doing, but by appointing a guardian, in writing, to see to his well being were I no longer able to.

That was my condition when Ben, whose fondness for cards resembled my father's but was milder, started holding all-male Tuesday night poker games, which banished Emily for the evening, but drew Libro like the smell of a biscuit in my pocket. I knew it was Tuesday when Libro, returning from his evening stroll, stopped belligerently on the second floor, refusing to come home with me. He sniffed Ben's door, then knocked as only a boxer can. A very indulgent Ben admitted him. Kaya looked up from her pillow and started to rise, seeing a friend, but Libro was not interested in Kaya. Deferring to him, Kaya sighed and lay down again. He was interested in the chip-laden table, where six boisterous males sat holding full houses or busted hands. After he circled the table, stopping at each player, inhaling testosterone, he walked to the door, ready to leave.

This behavior actually worried me a bit. For human companionship, Libro had me, increasingly open-hearted and constant, as well as my circle of close female friends, whom I thought of as his "aunties." And a grand lot they were, too. Olga, who took him to coffee shops in Spanish. Julie, who agreed to be listed in my will as Libro's guardian. Elayne, who organized a site for boxer rescues in Los Angeles, and sent photos of her own versions of Libro. But he was attracted to masculinity. Were he a baby instead of a dog, the need for a balance of estrogen and testosterone in his environment might have been more certain. Still, I wondered. Did he need a man in his life?

Did I?

# 4

## Citidog at the Seashore

*I was born by the sea and I have noticed that
all the great events of my life have taken place by
the sea. My first idea of movement, of the dance,
certainly came from the rhythm of the waves.*
—Isadora Duncan

After many, many months, a tidy sum of Yankee dollars had traveled from the pockets of customers to the tills of bookshops, to the computer screens and coffers of publishers, then to literary agents, then to the writer. Libro and I had accumulated the first nest egg I'd ever had, kept safely at the local Banco Popular. At the bank, he elicited a jaunty "*Hola, Libro*" greeting from the manager and he stood up on his rear legs to reach the teller's window, flapping his ears and extending his tongue toward the piles of money there. If anyone complained, which few people did, I merely said he had an account with the bank, which was true.

I was saving for our mutual old age, which I could barely imagine. I was past the midpoint of a human life span. I wondered if they allowed dogs as residents in the Hebrew Home for the Aged, where I'd always pictured myself in a black negligee and orthopedic shoes having sex with lovers who were old in both senses of the word. Though we were still far from retirement or decrepitude, Libro and I were approaching summer in a city prone to heat waves, where air conditioners kept us alive but sealed in the apartment. Knowing how Libro suffered on sizzling sidewalks and how long it had been since I'd had a real vacation, I said "yes" when the friend of a friend told me about an unexpectedly available Long Island beach rental for the month of August. My friend's friend had fallen in love with a California man and was willing to forgo East Coast sand and surf for love in freezing San Francisco. Dipping into the nest egg, I helped her out.

"You will love this place," I whispered into Libro's floppy ear. "You can run around without your leash."

The brindled boxer boy eyed the green-and-white canvas tote that was his travel bag and immediately went to wait at the apartment door. We were not actually on the verge of departure—this was only preparation, a pack-your-bathing-suit-and-don't-forget-the-sunscreen alert—but although he had many virtues, comprehension of time was not his strong suit. For Libro, today and now were all that existed. Some habits and phobias indicated that there had indeed been a yesterday, but it was quite well faded, while tomorrow made no sense. This was all philosophically instructive to me, but left him stranded at the door in a time warp.

A few days later, on the first of the month, we actually did leave, in a borrowed green Subaru whose high back seat caused some gimpy-legged difficulty. The capacious trunk space held a month's worth of kibble and canned food, vitamins, medicines, water bottles, tick sprays, shampoos, bowls, blankets, toys, doggy bed—and a slim assortment of shorts and bathing suits for me. Bound for a paradise of sea, surf and salty air, woman and dog—nostrils flared, anticipating solitude and nature—crept through the tollbooth on the Throgs Neck Bridge.

Libro sat upright on his haunches in the back seat, looking out the window, registering the roar of trucks and the impatient honking of horns on the highway. The tollbooth agent looked at him as I handed over our urban exit fee and asked, "Is that a dog?"

"I think so."

Some of the cars we chugged neck and neck with on the Expressway out to Long Island, exiting alongside our Subaru onto route 27 heading toward the eastern end, also had dogs in their back seats. Some had more than one. I imagined all of us—the Dalmatian in the red Camaro, the mastiff in the black MG, even the fluffy white creampuffs yipping in the battered Volvo—throwing and fetching sticks at sunset on the beach, looking a lot like the Kennedy clan playing touch football in Hyannis. Then I imagined myself alone with Libro at some place like Louse Point, my arms around him in quiet contemplation as sunset darkened the water and lights came on in the gray clapboard cottages nearby.

You do like to share your favorite places in the world with loved ones. The eastern end of Long Island is a part of the world I have known since I was in high school, when it was mostly a smallish, kind of funky potato-growing agricultural area, site of a productive fishing industry, inexpensive refuge for painters and writers, many of whom lived there year-round, and a well-kept secret as a summertime beach community. This was long before a poisoned ecology caused the sea bass to disappear, before potato fields were turned into private golf courses, before McMansions, bling, Starbucks, designer clothes, malls, and every other manifestation of "development."

Although people like me could barely afford to visit that former paradise for a weekend now, I could mark the stages of my life by things that had happened and people I had known on Long Island from year to year—the "lost" virginity in my best friend's family house in Sag Harbor; the sea trout caught at night from the shore at Long Beach where a Brit named Peter had taught me that skill, among others, and the culinary challenge of inventing sea trout recipes for weeks; the famous writer in his large ocean-view house with tennis court who used his name to jump a line of diners at Gossman's pier, inciting my revolutionary, egalitarian rage; the marriages and divorces of friends; the group rentals with their individually marked food in the refrigerators; and now, a place all our own, for a short time, just for me and Libro. The glamorous mother of my high school friend, the Brit and the famous writer were all dead. I was glad Libro was there.

After many hours on the road, we arrived at the house, which sat on a dead end lane. In daylight, I knew, we would see Accabonac Harbor a few feet away and on a clear day, the farther shore, with the unprepossessing house that once belonged to the Abstract Expressionist painters Jackson Pollock and Lee Krasner staring back at us. For now, all was quiet and dark. I was glad to have a bodyguard named Libro, although at the moment he acted more like a dog cooped up too long in a car—jumping down when I let him out, spinning in circles and peeing on all the bushes around the front door.

I remembered a house in the mountains of Massachusetts, decades before, where I'd lived alone during the summer that the harrowing film of Truman Capote's *In Cold Blood* came out. Far though it was from the killing fields of Kansas, that white colonial three-bedroom house in the Berkshires creaked ominously at night and the branches of huge oak and maple trees scraped at the windows. City Girl with something to prove, I tried to be brave. I would not be imprisoned by fear; I would not assume that the unfamiliar would kill me; I would not be a wimp.

Night after night, I lay in bed, listening to the creaks and scrapes, a blanket over my head like the most timid five-year-old. After an exhausting week, I found a solution that would not involve confessing my problem to anyone. I had a tape recorder with me and somehow I acquired a tape of a barking dog. Before daring to go to bed, I carried the "barking dog" through all the downstairs rooms, then put out the lights and climbed the stairs. Since technology had not yet provided the endless loop, my "dog" only "barked" for an hour, but that was sufficient to bring me peace of mind and untroubled sleep.

Now I had the real thing.

Taking in stride what I considered the astonishing fact that we merely opened a door and walked inside instead of climbing four flights of stairs at home, Libro investigated the beach house with the thoroughness of Inspector Clouseau. While I turned on all the lights, he looked under the beds and in all the closets. It was a very simple place, just a one-story cottage with the barest of furnishings, including white muslin draped over each of several living-room chairs and a 1950s Formica table in the kitchen. While I checked for soap and towels in the bathroom, he pushed the shower curtain aside and surveyed the tub. After turning on an outside spotlight, I gave the car's headlights a rest and carried Libro's fluffy dog bed from the car into the living room, careful to close the screen door behind me. If you say "country" to me, I say "bugs."

Libro's bed went in front of a white fireplace, which I thought made quite a nice tableau, though surely August would not require a lit fire. He ignored his bed, but not his food bowl, which I placed atop newspapers on the kitchen floor, lest we be liable for a lost deposit due to kibble stains. He was not a neat eater, but I could hardly criticize because neither was I.

We went to bed at last, he settling down in the living room, I in the bedroom, with the window open and a fresh salty breeze blowing. I fell asleep immediately. Not long afterward, toenails clicked on bare wood floors and Libro was beside my bed, which stood high off the ground. A lifted paw rested beside my foot. A deep sigh echoed through the room. I turned on the bedside lamp. A pathetic face importuned me.

"No, Libro. Go to your bed."

Libro had proven himself an impossible, restless bedmate in general, allowed into my bed only when there was no other option, as in "dog friendly" hotel rooms in California, where friendliness was encouraged by the lack of a separate place for the dog to sleep. This beach house had many options, including three bedrooms. Eventually, worn out by moving Libro back to his own his bed, offering bribery by biscuit for staying put, I did just close my eyes and hope for the best. In the morning, a snoring dog lay on the rag rug on the floor near my bed.

We were at the beach, in nature, a place where every star in the sky was visible, where our little lane had virtually no traffic going by at night; where, come daylight, Libro could wander a bit by himself. Although another house sidled up to the one we were staying in on one side, the other side fronted open space, a patch of woods. I had no idea what I would do if Libro went wandering off and returned with some putrid catch—a raccoon, say, or even a snake—between those scissor-sharp teeth, but I was willing to find out. A dog is, after all, an animal and an animal's métier is the natural world. Though he had adapted well to the hypercivilized world of neighbors, television sets, and even vacuum cleaners and my computer's printer—none of which his DNA had prepared him for—I was now returning the favor by introducing him to "the wild." That "the wild" was a place where you sat in traffic jams if you ventured onto the main roads, or paid $5 for a cup of coffee, mattered less than the fact that I could go barefoot all day and hear crickets at night. It was closer to nature than our urban life was.

In the morning, I opened the door and held it for him. Libro waited for me. I indicated he should go out by himself. But he had not seen all the movies I had, where the canine bounds away from the house to do whatever canines do in nature and returns in due course and as a matter of course. Although he had visited people in country houses whose dogs wandered and returned on their own, Libro didn't seem to understand that mode of behavior was now possible for him. Or was expected of him. He disbelieved.

"Out," I said, as invitingly as possible, pointing to the great outdoors.

He went out. I let the door close and turned to the dishes in the sink. One coffee cup and two breakfast spoons later, there came a terrible scratching—Libro at the screen door.

"Go for a walk," I said, dishtowel and cup in hand. "Don't go far, just down the road. Go pee."

He had torn a hole in the screen.

He stopped scratching and lay down with nary a sound. I went back to the dishes. When I checked, Libro was in the same position, waiting.

"Don't you want a walk?"

He knew the word. He raised his head. He knew many words. But I knew more, and it came to me after a while that the word Libro was waiting for was "leash."

"You want your leash?"

He did.

We walked together to the end of the lane just as we walked at home, with me holding the leash in my hand. We turned left at the paved road, stayed well to the shoulder as cars whizzed by, and eventually came to a farm stand. A large unleashed setter barked to let the world—and us—know that she was there and that another canine had approached. I unhooked Libro's leash to encourage him to romp with the setter, which he did, well away from the road, while I introduced myself to the proprietor and her daughter, then inspected the luscious zucchini, corn, blueberries, and freshly cut sunflowers.

Obliquely, I saw him race past a burlap sack full of corn ears and stop to lift his leg.

"No! Libro, no!"

My "no" was too late—a stained river of urine trickled down the sack, seeping into the corn. The stand owner laughed, but I offered to pay for the damage. She refused. As we walked away, Libro trotted in the direction of the house while I hung my head.

Denial is a wonderful thing. It keeps us hoping in the face of all evidence to the contrary. I knew that Libro was not exactly fond of water. We had survived quite a few New York winters together and I had watched as, on snow-covered sidewalks, he tried to get from our doorstep to the corner without letting his paws touch the ground for too long. On rainy days, he barely tolerated the great urban outdoors, ducking into any available doorway every few steps, startling doormen, dripping on the marble floors of apartment buildings and refusing to brave the street again until the rain let up. I knew that he could swim, however, because early in our cohabitation, I'd urged him into the nearby Hudson River while I kept hold of his leash, just for information. But even on those splendid California beaches we had visited, Libro treated the ocean as a border not to be approached, the forbidden frontier at the edge of the real world, which was terra firma, dry sand.

His aversion to wetness was in part structural, the way his body was made. His paws were not webbed and most of his weight was in his chest, which had expanded by many inches in his second year, inflating like a balloon and remaining so from then on. Libro in a body of water had little chance of being a swimmer unless he made an effort. If nature had its way, he tipped beneath the surface, head first, dragged under by the weight of his chest, tail aloft like a buoy. On the rare occasions I had witnessed this sight, he had righted himself and looked at me in that puzzled way: "What the hell just happened?" Then he paddled very quickly to safety.

Still, I persisted in imagining us at the beach, frolicking like Girl and Spot in any Coppertone ad, and I put my imagination to the test the next morning. Climbing into the car for Libro was simple. Taking in the scenery as he sat in the back seat with the windows down and a sea breeze blowing as I drove along Old Stone Highway was fun. I turned onto Louse Point Road, past a row of cottages, around a curve, past brightly colored overturned canoes and finally came to the small parking lot at the end, on a point surrounded by water. Libro bounded out of the car. I kicked off my shoes and walked onto the narrow beach. He followed.

So far, everything was familiar to Libro, including sand, the surface of those California beaches and some beach volleyball courts back home in Riverside Park. Though sand scratched his paws and he'd rather haul kids on skateboards three miles along paved paths in the park than endure it, he was being a good sport on this bright morning, curiosity about a new place superseding any mild discomfort. I believed he could transcend his past habits and preferences.

I lay the nice yellow blanket I had removed from one of the closets on the sand and Libro sat on it. It was still early, but I put up the green-and-white striped umbrella I'd found in the basement and made sure the little prince was safely in its shade. Then I walked to the water. He got up and followed. We advanced. By the time I was calf-deep, Libro had stopped and was looking belligerent. I urged him forward. He refused. I sent him back to the blanket. He refused. I sighed and looked to the sky.

He would not follow me in; he would not stay on shore. We rarely had power struggles like this one, mostly because he was such a good dog and because I treated him fairly, being agreeable and not arbitrary in exercising control. I'd become a dog person, at last. But the stalemate with our feet in the water was not easily resolved. I morphed into a dominatrix, demanding that he wait on the blanket, under "his" umbrella if he wouldn't paddle beside me in the water. He went back to home base. I swam out alone. But the din on the beach drew me back. Libro was racing up and down, barking. I came out of the water to reassure him that my arms and legs were fluttering, not flailing—I made the motions on land, like a madwoman—that though I swam nearly out of his sight, I would return to terra firma and to him: "I will never leave you. I will never leave you."

Libro didn't believe me. Rescue was needed. This apparently required racing up and down the beach and howling to gather the troops. If I swam, he howled; if I came out of the water, he lay down on the blanket like a good dog. It was a very hot day.

I got angry. I got comforting. I got threatening. I gave him biscuits and lectures and made a lot of promises. Nothing worked. I went back into the water and he went back to sounding the alarm until, fearful of being evicted by the others enjoying the day on the beach, I took him home.

On subsequent days, I tried leaving him in the car with the windows safely lowered while I went for a swim, but he barked there, too—a demanding, panic-stricken bark—while I, the love of his life, entered the water and confronted what he continued to believe was certain death. Eventually, he had to stay behind in the rental house, even on the hottest days, with all the floor fans encircling him, if I wanted a swim. We had reached the first serious rift in our perfect coupling, our first recognition that my pleasures were not always his, nor his mine. The dynamic duo might have, at times, separate roads to bliss.

Surveying paradise through Libro's eyes, I could see that much was missing. There was no Kaya to play tug with, no Ben to wrestle with, no garbage cans or people asleep on park benches and no pedestrian traffic to entertain him. In fact, except for the actual town of East Hampton, where we rarely ventured because I was too smart and too experienced at "in season" living to expose us to city manners, city people, and row upon row of city stores, there were few sidewalks at all. I imagined him thinking, *Where is everybody?* The "everybody" might have included the homeless people, of whom we saw nary a one and perhaps the Spanish-speaking people like Olga our neighbor or the soccer-playing, extended families who picnicked in Riverside Park. There were actually Spanish-speaking people not far away, but Libro never got to meet them because the gardeners, housemaids, and cleaners, whose work occupied them from sunup to sundown, lived in their own *barrio* and, except for the odd garage sale, did not mix with "summer people," among whom I most uncomfortably now found myself.

More troublesome, perhaps, was this: the very same dog who slept peacefully through ambulance sirens and drunken revelers on the streets of Manhattan sat, after sunset, entirely alert inside the screened-in French doors in the rear of the beach house, staring out into the darkness. His nose quivered and his brow knitted; and every once in a while, at the sound, say, of a cricket, his ears went up and his muscles tensed.

"What's *out* there?"

Would a tape of a barking dog be of any help?

But just around the corner from the house was Libro's version of paradise. The Springs General Store was a busy place, from early breakfast 'til closing time. It had a gravel parking lot and an unused old gas pump outside, a wooden porch, home-cooked food, and a certain mystique, being, in folklore at least, the place where Jackson Pollock traded a painting for beers.

The noise and the smell of customers' car exhausts might have bothered more bucolic neighbors, but to Libro, it reeked of home. Sports cars and family cars and pickup trucks pulled in and out. Couples and singles and fishermen and sailors and children and dogs arrived and left. The humans went inside the store, purchased a flashlight or a corned beef sandwich, came out and drove away or they stayed a while on the porch, lounging in Adirondack chairs and, especially on Sundays, reading the *New York Times*. Evenings were more homey and local, the lights blazing on the porch in the black night reminiscent of Hopper's diner in a purely American landscape.

While Libro lay on the porch steps, at breakfast, lunch, dinner time or late at night, whenever I would allow him to drag me there, a vast swarm of humanity banged the store's screen door open and closed as they went inside for coffee refills or ice cream pops, came out onto the porch talking on cell phones and even, occasionally, smoking cigarettes. This was fun; this was action; this was living. *Eso es vivir.*

He never left willingly; I always had to drag Libro away. Knowing him as well as I did, I understood that the scene at the general store provided the two things Libro loved most in the world: food and an audience.

My old friend Heather lived year-round in a town a few miles away, where she taught writing at the local college and helped gifted high-school students be-come Brontës and Dickinsons during the summer months. Heather is the most animal-loving person of everyone I know, always has been. Her first baby photographs show her sucking her thumb and clasp-ing the ear of Blackie, the family cocker spaniel for a "blankie." She spent a lifetime in rural settings, around horses, sheep, and dogs. Her current home, with Poco the Dalmatian and Poco's "other mother," included fish in an outdoor pond, several indoor cats of her own and a stray who had moved in, all of which meant I could never go visit her because I would seize up with asthma and Libro would seize up with murder.

Although Heather had tracked Libro's life with me from the moment he arrived, via telephone and email, we were taking the opportunity of a month within driving distance to hang out live and in person, *à trois*, as much as we could. She came for lunch, bringing

Poco. I made tuna salad with real tuna fish, caught by some of the few remaining fishermen the day before in nearby Montauk. We talked about teaching jobs and novel writing while the dogs ignored each other, which disappointed me, since I thought of Poco as Libro's cousin. Then, again, coexisting in the same space without much conversation might be the way one does treat a cousin. At any rate, after they'd ascertained that neither was a killer, the way dogs do, Poco wandered away down the lane and into the fields, leashless and without human companionship, like a "real dog." Libro remained at our feet, listening intently to the conversation and eyeing the tuna salad.

One afternoon, nearly midmonth, I tried playing tennis, a lifetime pleasure only slightly diminished by the slower speed and weaker overhead that came willy nilly with "advancing" years. Or not. I thought of Martina Navratilova and vowed to do weights and squats 'til I tumbled into my grave; but for now, merely swinging the racket and connecting with the ball would be enough. Just down the road, past the farm market, scene of our disgrace, were shady local tennis courts, well kept and under-utilized. Libro watched as I sat on the bed tying my sneakers and picked up my rackets. His tail wagged.

No more lying abed, fanned like a sultan. We were going somewhere! *Eso es vivir* again!

I opened the kitchen screen door, cradled my rackets and went out, leash in hand. Libro aimed for the general store, but I pulled him in the other direction.

A pickup truck was parked near the courts with a large shaggy black dog resting in its bed. I wondered if Libro was registering the variety of canine lifestyles our sojourn was revealing: some wandered freely in and out of the lanes, onto the porch of the general store and back toward the wooded areas and then, presumably, to homes where they either resided in the yard or were allowed in the house; other dogs remained in their front yards untethered, but wound up to be alarm systems if strangers came near; some rode in convertibles, a small one had been spied in the basket of a bicycle; others lounged in pickup trucks. The shaggy dog raised one lazy eye, glanced at Libro, who must have seemed like Little Lord Fauntleroy with his collar and leash, and went back to snoozing.

The truck's young driver, who looked no older than eighteen and suggested, for a moment, the possibility of my turning into Mrs. Robinson, offered to hit a few balls with me, a more generous offer than the opportunity to play Mrs. Robinson. We took the tennis court nearest a high wire fence, where, although I would have preferred using him as a ball boy, I tied Libro up. He lay down peacefully and squinted in the sun.

I stretched and warmed up, unzipped the racket cover and hit a ball over the net. The guy on the other side hit it back nicely, though it was clear from his stance and musculature that he could have sent it hurtling out of my reach. And immediately, Libro was on his feet, barking. I told him to sit and be quiet, then hit another ball. He was sitting and not barking. But when the ball came back across the net toward me, he stood again and barked again. This was different from the beach bark, which had signaled panic and emergency and was meant to rouse the entire populace. On the tennis courts, where the "enemy" appeared to be a single projectile, not the vast briny deep, Libro was slightly more measured and decidedly aimed at the hapless fellow who was sending the fuzzy yellow ball in my direction. This was a "cut-it-out" bark, but an irritating distraction nonetheless. After apologies on my part and a good sport effort on the other side of the net—while his dog remained uninvolved in these shenanigans—we quit and Libro and I, leashed together, went home again, making sure to cross the highway to avoid the farm stand.

Julie, my city friend, owned a house nearby, plus a twelve-foot-long wooden sailboat. To save us from the tedium of staying home, lounging outdoors on chaises or indoors in front of large fans, or visiting the general store—the only activities that did not irritate Libro and make my life miserable—she offered to take us both sailing. Being an extremely safety-minded sailor, Julie had two requirements: Libro needed a life jacket and we had to practice on dry land before taking to the water. The first was harder than it seemed. For a doggy life jacket, he and I got in the car—that was fun—went past the local dump (another place that amused him) and onto the crowded highway, out to the nearest pet store, in Montauk. Libro was in his element, begging biscuits, receiving *oohs* and *ahs* and ear scratches, blubbering all over the salespeople, but no lifejackets, which had been sold out for weeks. Thus began a trek up and down the most congested roads on the East Coast, visiting shops farther and farther from home base. Many were out of stock; others had jackets that would not close around his handsome chest, making him look like a 300-pound man poured into a tiny bikini. Eventually, halfway back to Manhattan, we found a bright yellow safety jacket exactly the right size and Libro actually let me put it on him.

Julie led us, the next day, through all possible catastrophes. Libro might jump at a gull as it flew overhead and fall into the water. He might get tangled in the mainsheet lines. He might capsize the boat. So we divided responsibilities: Libro was mine, the handles atop his yellow garment exactly positioned so I could grab him and tow him to shore, assuming I could swim with seventy pounds bobbing along with me; the vessel was Julie's. She was a bit worried about Libro's paws scratching the exquisitely varnished oak decking, but neither of us could think of a way to ensure that would not happen.

It rained nonstop for two days. I used the time to do some writing and to instruct Libro in what I knew of sailing etiquette—duck when the captain says "coming about" and do every single thing she tells us to. He listened with his head cocked, a sign of good concentration. When the sun came out, *Swallow*, as she was called, awaited, just off the ramp at the end of our lane, with Julie already aboard, unsnapping and unfurling. Libro and I waded toward her.

"Up," I said and Libro, in his canary yellow jacket, jumped into the boat, avoiding the nice wood decking. He went immediately to the belly of the small sailboat and lay down while I did everything Julie told me to do. I sat exactly where she told me to sit, ready to let go of the centerboard. Up came the sails, and off we went into the bay. We tacked. We came about. A breeze rocked us gently. The shore receded.

"Look, Libro," I said, assuming that the sight of the land moving away might interest him. But Libro, at my feet, was fast asleep. His eyelids fluttered with dreaming and he emitted small, satisfied whimpers.

We sailed on, all the way to within reach of the beach at Louse Point. Julie, as captain, maneuvered the vessel with confidence and expertise, self-assured with the mainsheet in her hand and her eyes on the horizon. Birds squawked overhead. The breeze picked

up. We tacked and came about some more and then
we headed back. As I pulled the centerboard up in
shallow water, Libro opened one eye.

"You missed it. You missed the whole sail."

He rose and jumped off without scratching a thing,
racing ahead of me through reedy, mucky shallows for
safe dry land.

Nightly, I examined Libro for deer ticks, the bane of
summer frolic on the Eastern Shore. That he was not a
shaggy dog made the task easy. That I was not a shaggy
dog was useful too, but not prophylactic. On a late August afternoon, after a quick trip to swim at Louse Point
without Libro, soaped up under the outdoor shower, I
found a large black spot on my belly. I rushed inside,
assembled the required magnifying glass, alcohol and
tweezers. Libro, snuggled on an outdoor chaise, followed me, sensing alarm. I got the bastard out of my
flesh and wrapped it in a tissue. At home, in Manhattan, it would have been a five minute cab ride to the
nearest emergency room, but I was in "the wilds" and,
determined to get the critter checked out, had to drive
to the Southampton hospital, twenty-five miles away
on the most congested two-lane road in the world.

Libro whimpered as I slammed the newly patched
screen door behind me. When I returned, hours later,
antibiotics in hand, he sniffed through my clothes at
the reddening welt on my belly and, looking sorrowful

and compassionate, apparently forgot for the first time in his life that his dinner was being served a tad late that day.

As August drew to a close, I noticed that I had entirely relinquished my dreams of sunset swims together, more appropriate to golden retrievers and labs than to intellectual boxers, more derived from the paintings of Thomas Eakins and the watercolors of children's storybooks than from the actual experience of living with Libro. I accepted him, again, for who he was. He was a city dog living with a city woman surrounded by things that puzzled or unnerved him and sometimes elicited the same responses from me. I was, however, capable of explaining a few things: a deer on the road, caught, cinematically, in the car's headlights one night; or a rowboat pulled from the shore by a tanned young couple as we passed by on an afternoon walk, settling into the water, where the couple climbed in and the entire unit traveled off and away.

"Those are large dogs," I said, in the first instance. And "it's a car that goes on water" in the second.

The next-to-last day of the month, I'd nearly finished packing Libro's gear, including the bulky life jacket and all my things, including quite a few treasures acquired at Saturday afternoon yard sales. I invited Heather for a last swim. Close to sunset, Libro, Heather and I drove to the beach on the bay, while osprey squawked overhead and the dank marsh smell filled my nose with pleasure and Libro's with dread. I had forgiven him all his peculiarities, including his refusal to indulge me by swimming. While he and I waited in our street clothes on the sand, Heather went in the water, wearing snorkeling goggles that made her look more like a mad aviator than an experienced swimmer. Libro watched intently, ready to spring, just as he watched the bees on the terrace at home. His ears were half-lifted, anticipating the sound of danger. Heather stroked gracefully back and forth and waved and then, as she swam toward shore, dove and disappeared beneath the surface of the water.

Libro narrowed his eyes as though adjusting his vision would bring the sight of Heather back. Then he looked at me. I said Heather was okay and tried to get my tongue around "snorkel" in a way Libro might understand, but before I could form a syllable, he had raced in, eyes fixed on the spot where Heather had submerged. She, however, had been moving underwater. Just when he reached the depth where his chest grazed the water's surface, he stopped, lowered his head, and stuck his nose into the water. Up came Heather's head, long blonde hair dripping like a mermaid's. Her giggles and mine echoed across the bay. She stood. And up came Libro's head, eyes closed, nose sputtering. Would that I'd had an underwater camera to capture the moment when Heather opened her eyes behind her goggles to find Libro's dark muzzle filling her vision, nostrils quivering.

"Oh, good dog," I said, from shore as they walked toward me, Libro licking Heather's hand, snorting salt water and trying to shake himself dry at the same time. "Now we can go home."

He bounded from the car onto the sidewalk in front of our building, intoxicated by the concrete beneath his paws and other dogs' pee, the reek of garbage cans in that flat, quivering nose so recently exposed to the horrors of the deep. With unmistakable joy, he returned to climbing four flights of stairs, the lullaby of horns honking and air conditioners blasting at night, the safety of everything familiar and loved. I was sure that the messages he left in the street for his peers were full of boasting about surviving the torture of a month in the Hamptons.

# 5

# Calamities

*I always thought it mattered, to know what is the worst possible thing that can happen to you, to know how you can avoid it, to not be drawn by the magic of the unspeakable.*

—Amy Tan

My life with Libro was wonderful but not without worry. We had already weathered two serious assaults on our merely mortal bodies. Mine came first.

The first time I had an inkling that there was more to me than met the eye was in a shoe store when I was very young. The salesman fitting me stuck my feet into a machine; I looked down—and there was the world beneath the flesh, my sinews and bones. I think the machine was a fluoroscope and in it, my bones glowed neon green. Its ostensible purpose had something to do with sizing the shoes. For a few dozen years, that was all I knew about my innards, which I carried around in blissful ignorance, except for an occasional suspicion that they were neon green. My tonsils were removed, but who knew what color or shape tonsils were, or even where they resided before they were gone and re-placed by ice cream licked to ease the soreness? As my neon green foot bones grew, so did breasts and hair in hitherto bare places. Around that time, I was informed about "parts" south of my tonsils that would—and did—bleed monthly and require strange contraptions to keep in check. No ice cream for that, just a pam-phlet, a drawing in "health education" class where boys tittered and teachers blushed. That part of my anatomy was an inverted triangle anchored by ovaries on either side, connected by tubes and anchored, at the upside-down apex, by a passageway leading out to the world and in to this theater of wonders or travails known as uterus or, in a more literary way, womb. Un-like say, tonsils, these body parts were very personal, female, mysterious.

"The man plants a seed in the woman's womb and a baby grows." Thus said my very precise mother, ne-glecting to allow as how man and woman were touch-ing or even in the same neighborhood. Aside from leaving me to picture a seed flying through the air, say, from dad's office, along the streets and into the kitchen, where mom waited, this feat of engineering meant, to the young me, that "womb" was full of something like garden earth and to speculate that the growing baby probably resembled a tree.

The word "womb" was everywhere, as I acquired an education, which came to include not only a clearer picture of how the seed was planted and the baby grew—I did, after all, attend a fancy women's college—but of many kinds of poetic meaning that accrued to it. "Womb" meant safety and shelter. Mary's womb, in some accounts, was akin to an altar at which humankind worshipped. But *hyster*, the Greek word for that place, was also the root of the word hysteria, which led to much theorizing in various texts over many centuries, about how the inverted triangle and its casing made women crazy.

Along came Sigmund Freud, Erik Erickson and feminism, all engaging in lively debate about how this particular body part affected not only the self-image of female people, but their ability to work, study, head up a work crew or represent a constituency in Congress. "Inner space" was Erickson's description, based on studies showing boy children playing with blocks to form projecting edifices while their sisters made enclosures. "Inner space," to some smart and now anonymous feminist, sounded suspiciously like a hole in the head. Bah, humbug, said I, it's just tissue and nerve endings, the rag and bone shop of the body, the abode of neither angels nor devils.

Then my womb got sick, though it never bothered to tell me it was. The doctors and the laboratories with their microscopes and glass slides discovered that certain cells were misbehaving and they called it cancer.

They say dogs can smell cancer and if I had believed that, I would have been—for the first time in our life together—disappointed in Libro. Actually, what scientists know is that dogs can be *taught* to smell cancer. Unfortunately, for all the things Libro had been taught, from how to keep his nether parts away from the television camera to how to sit quietly on the couch when I was working, it had never occurred to me to add cancer smelling to the list. Why should it? Our life together was nothing but pleasure and joy in the form of park outings, sloppy kisses, cafes, car rides, laughter, telepathy, and miracles.

The sense of telepathy and miracles had come to me more slowly than the obvious, simple pleasures. I could date what I'd call the growing spiritual nature of my connection to Libro from the day Sister Veronica appeared like an apparition in the park and I'd said "makes you believe in God doesn't it?" as a laugh. Or not as a laugh. The language came awkwardly to my lips. I shared it with virtually no one, but the truth was, Libro had become more than my own personal version of Harvey the Rabbit, that invisible friend to Jimmy Stewart in the movie. More than my buddy, more than my Saturday night date, I thought of him as a brown angel. What else could he be, having arrived as a gift, neither requested nor understood, and having remained as a constant, unconditional source of love and happiness?

For the first time, I noticed the number of angels I had collected in my home over the years. There were two small stone cherubs on the terrace, one playing a harp and another blowing a kiss. A dramatic carved and painted wooden female figure with enormous white *Angels in America* wings, wearing a turquoise dress and clutching an hourglass stood on my desk. She'd been made in Mexico, where reminders of time running out are as common to the culture as the sense of limitless time is to ours, and where *El Dia de Los Muertos*, The Day of the Dead, is a national holiday, an orgiastic celebration of the spirits of departed ancestors. The tin angel in a bright red dress looking down from my bedroom wall had also been *hecho en Mexico*, while a more domestically made green and white straw angel hung from an embroidered thread off a bookshelf.

Superstitious? Obviously. In need of all the help I could get? To be sure. But the point was, given all this magical protection, not to mention the presence of my brown angel, I believed nothing bad could possibly be in the cards for either of us. I'd even become convinced that Libro's gimpy leg was a good thing, an imperfection that saved him from being an arrogant prince and saved me from being consort to an arrogant prince, something any woman who has hung around with brilliant, successful men has had some experience with.

I could not blame Libro for not smelling cancer—he had never met it. When I tried to imagine what cancer smelled like, all I could think of was pickles. I asked my friends. "Ashes," Heather said on the telephone. "Rotting fruit," offered Olga.

My worst nightmare to date, probably not so different from anyone else's, had been that I would find myself seriously ill and alone. I had cancer, which I believed qualified as serious, but I was surely not alone. If friends are chosen family, there were enough of them nearby and even more within traveling distance to fill a large airplane. Olga was on the first floor of my building, Maria on the second. Julie was a few blocks away. Heather was on Long Island. These were the kind of friends you can count on. And I had Libro, although for a heartbeat, while I threw myself into research and doctor visits and insurance forms and surgery scheduling, I lost the "brown angel" in my mind and he became objectified as merely "the dog."

What to do about "the dog" while I was hospitalized and surgeried and then for the recuperative weeks afterward? People with Mom-Dad-Dick-and-Jane-and-Spot lives probably find the question less daunting than I did. I forgot for a moment that I had faced "what to do with the dog" many times, although I had not thought of it in those heartless terms. He'd had the rotating care of my neighbors when I went to visit my father in Florida and Olga's overnight supervision during my brief business trips, all of which had left him apparently unscarred. When Annette the theatrical producer and Eve the stockbroker, who were happy to have a dog around as they recovered from the death of theirs, offered to take care of him, I readily agreed.

The doctor wore beige corduroy trousers under his white coat as he saved my life. That was the last thing I saw before anesthesia carried me away, although I also remember feeling that Libro was somewhere outside the hospital, standing guard. I was lucky. All the cancer had been cut away. The laws of gastroenterology dictated that I had to wait several days in my hospital bed before I could enjoy solid food. Enraged at the only sustenance allowed—lime Jell-O—I threatened to sell my body for food in the hospital corridors. That told the doctors and nurses that I was well on the road to recovery.

Five days later, with friends hovering on either side, I went up four flights of stairs very, very slowly, to an apartment without Libro. Maria cooked me lasagna. Roland brought newspapers. Gretchen sent her cleaning person. A masseuse came with aromatic oils. Peter Pan from California, who just happened to be in town, brought flowers and helped refill the tank of the humidifier, which I was not allowed to lift. Winter roared outside and the radiators hissed steam around the clock. I wanted Libro.

The deft surgery had left a stapled and bandaged half-moon wound, "below the bikini line," I'd been assured, though not dying trumped scar-showing bikinis in my hierarchy of needs. Ever the Mistress of the Revels, I'd photographed the stapled smiley-face on my bare skin and created a photograph to use as a thank you card to the legions who had helped. But what, I worried, would my rambunctious boxer boy do if he got affectionate or playful within striking distance of the wound?

A dog trainer was suggested. He came ten days after my return from the hospital, just before Libro was to come home.

"From the minute he walks in," the trainer said, "you have to exaggerate your frailty."

We held a dogless dress rehearsal. I lay on the sofa in a nightgown and robe, with the back of my hand across my forehead and I said, in the softest voice I have ever used:

"Hello, Libro."

*La Dame Aux Camellias.* My mother, a fan of operas with pale frail dying women at the center of the drama, would have loved it.

"Weaker," the trainer said, "more frail."

"Hello"—barely audible—"Libro."

The doorbell rang downstairs, prompting the trainer to step into a corner as though he could disappear from the room. I heard four human feet climbing the stairs, four canine feet racing, as I lay center stage in my Elizabeth Barrett Browning pose. Libro brought his own theatrics.

The apartment door opened, Libro rushed in, pulling Eve, followed by Annette. He looked larger than I remembered, and his coat was greasy, as though someone had been feeding him flaxseed capsules or barbecued ribs. About ten feet from the couch, he stopped. Looked around. Sniffed. Ignored the trainer. Eve unleashed him and we all held our breaths as I began to form my whispery lines in my throat.

But "hello, Libro" was unnecessary and so too was the fainting pose. Libro walked but did not run. Did not leap. Did not tear at my stitches. Did nothing but maintain eye contact and arrive beside the couch, sniff the wound gently and lie down on the floor immediately beside me, a barricade.

A barricade he remained for all the days that followed, leaving my side only to attend to his own needs—two meals, some medications, and three walks a day with a rotating cast of escorts. I had made a chart, organizing my care and his: one person a day to visit and accompany him to the street. Allowing, as being *in extremis* forces you to, for the idiosyncrasies and neuroses of some people—phobic about illness, as I too had been for most of my life, able to send long-stemmed yellow tulips or cute cards, but not to appear in person—I had managed to summon enough friends and near-friends to cover the days.

I strengthened enough to leave the apartment, first with a human to lean on, eventually alone with Libro. Although it was clearly unnecessary to explain the circumstances to him, I did.

"We have to walk slowly, Libro. You can't pull on the leash. You can't chase any cats."

He knew. He knew.

Reentering the world, we encountered trouble. A four-year-old scrappy gray Lhasa apso with one damaged eye had been found in a junkyard and adopted by Olga, who named her Trixie. Libro did not like this turn of events one bit. When he saw Olga with Trixie in the street, instead of approaching excitedly as he had when Olga was all his, he turned his head away, ignoring the interloper. Later, he lay his body across the threshold of Olga's apartment so that she and Trixie could not enter.

As the days passed, I became nearly as strong as I had been before and my scar faded. I knew I was a wombless wonder but had no idea what that might mean. I did know that Libro's presence had something to do with my miraculous healing and I rewarded him amply for his help, with longer and longer walks and many, many treats. I'm sure he saw these things as nothing but proof that I was fun to be with again.

Still, I needed help. Libro was going to have a nanny. "Dog nanny needed" read the online ad I posted at Barnard and Columbia. Those nearby schools had, over the years, been a source of research assistants and helpers of many kinds. Most of the helpers turned into surrogate daughters, which meant that I supplied career or romance advice when asked, gave glamorous gifts, and offered a bed away from campus dormitories when things there got too stressful. One such young woman was the daughter of the man I'd gone to the Columbia Senior Prom with.

A series of students responded to my dog-nanny ad, all of them meeting the requirements of reliability, midday availability, and the athleticism necessary for an hour in the park with a hefty boxer. Plus, of course, a dog-loving nature, which hardly needed saying, since dog nannies made less per hour than their sister students who worked part time at data entry or in the student bookstore. The applicants, on the whole, were brilliant young women majoring in everything from art history to international affairs.

They "dared to use the f-word," as one of their T-shirts said, *f* meaning "feminist." Only one had a nose ring. I hired Jenny, a senior who had spent a semester doing volunteer work in Africa. She did not have a nose ring.

After one somewhat reluctant initial outing that left me behind, Libro treated Jenny like a sibling. He loved her and took her entirely for granted. She arrived week-days at noon, returned at two and invariably both came home bathed in sweat. If she was late, he paced. When the human calendar said Saturday or Sunday, she did not appear at all and he spent the better part of those afternoons sniffing under the door with expectation that seemed to me to turn to despair.

Jenny lasted through our second calamity. This time, it befell Libro.

We were in Straus Park one cold afternoon. The fountain was iced up, and there were no children or nannies to be seen. Libro stumbled and fell on the salt-strewn path. It took him a long time to get upright, even with my frantic help, and when he did, he couldn't put his weight on the "bad" leg. His high-pitched pained cries broke my heart, but they also brought help. I always said that emergencies are best had on city streets, where, contrary to popular belief,

strangers do stop to help, especially if you are a slim
five-foot-three female person with a large limping,
wincing boxer.

Two local building superintendents got us to the
vet's office, where a torn ligament was diagnosed. I
had to leave Libro overnight for surgical repair the
following morning. Although similar injuries occur
in young dogs, I took Libro's ruptured ligament as the
price of all the running, leaping, and pounding on
sidewalks he had done, all that climbing into and out
of rental cars and SUVs. *El precio de vivir.* The price
of living. Libro was middle-aged. Me, too. I had my
grandmother's bunion. My teeth were beginning to
require as much care as they'd needed when I was a
growing girl. Years of walking and chewing were taking their toll on me, too.

At home that night, I cooked dinner for myself
and ate without having a pair of amber eyes plead, or
a tongue reach out expectantly toward my plate. I
sighed the way Libro often did, hoping it was true
that fifty was the new forty; that sixty was the new
forty and that perhaps seventy. . . .

I tried to read, but the space where my body curved
into my waist seemed empty as I lay on the couch
with a book in my hand. I tried to sleep. Then I
found myself going down the stairs like a somnambu-
list, walking with some trepidation along the empty
dark street toward the vet's closed-up office, where

Libro was sleeping not in his soft bed, but in a cage. I stood outside, whispering "Everything will be okay" and "I will never leave you," until the sun came up. I was sure he heard me.

Libro came home after surgery with a cast on his leg, wrapped in red gauze, which made it look like he was dragging a Christmas stocking around with him. All along, I'd been collecting information about torn ligaments and aftercare from the experts in the dog run and the people who posted in online chat rooms, which were cyberspace dog runs. Many folks had lived through such injuries and surgeries and among those residing in New York, where staircases of four or five stories were common, I encountered a few martyrs. Some people had actually carried their dogs up and down the stairs after the operation, which was fine for male weight lifters or anyone with dachshunds and teacup Malteses, but not for boxers weighing over sixty pounds. Still, I read about women who had compassionately lifted their German shepherds or rottweilers and in the process, hurt themselves severely.

I loved Libro as much as anyone loved a dog, but I wasn't eager for a sprained back. Luckily, having a building to help raise the dog included having several strong young men as neighbors. For Ben in particular, it was no sweat to carry Libro up and down the stairs the first few days. Libro squirmed in Ben's arms, insulted, I believed, at being treated like a baby.

"Don't worry," I said. "Nobody can see you, and I promise I won't tell."

Jenny returned for the rest of the school year, playing indoors with Libro until his cast came off, then taking him out for careful walks that resembled the forays he had accompanied me on after my surgery. When she left us to prepare for job interviews, I worried about Libro's despair and the jarring effect of having a series of different caretakers, but still I posted another "dog nanny wanted" notice. Anna was only a sophomore, a slim blonde studying international relations, missing her dog at home in Colorado. She not only did her "job" walking Libro during the week, but, unlike the older and more ambitious Jenny, dropped by on weekends just to play with him. I was happy to share.

Now it was my father who was failing. He sat in a dark air-conditioned room in his Florida condo with the television set blaring, waiting for death to walk through the door. His heart was closing down. An aide came daily to check the oxygen tank beside the hospital bed that had been moved into his bedroom and the one in the den, where he sometimes watched the larger television set or played videotapes of the operas he and my mother had often enjoyed.

We talked every night. He always said "I love you" before he hung up.

By the beginning of September, he had been moved to a hospice, where people treated death like death, clear-eyed and uncurtained, head on, without euphemism or histrionics. My father had told me he was ready to go and at peace with the life he had led. He had told the hospice nurses that he would need a sunny room for a few days and after that, he would not care. A "do not resuscitate" order was in place.

On Labor Day weekend, right at the beginning of the season when animals were allowed to travel in airplanes to hot climates like Florida's, I packed for Libro and myself. This time, I needed nobody's permission to bring him. By now, his crate, the airport and the plane were unremarkable experiences for Libro. Not so the heavy humidity in the air when we landed in Florida and the strange, ghostly objects—hospital bed and oxygen tanks—around the place where we would sleep. Like any good dog, even though he was quite firmly a brown angel in my mind by now, Libro made sure he smelled every inch of the condo and then he stayed close, watching my face for tears he could lick away.

I sat on my father's bed in the hospice, holding his hand. With his other hand, he picked at his blankets. His eyes were closed. He didn't make a sound. The hospice workers said that he was nearing the end. His younger sister, who lived nearby, was there. For the sake of conversation, as we waited and watched, she asked me what I had been doing that morning. In fact, I had been hugging Libro and cleaning the condo, having the medical apparatus removed, opening dusty drawers and emptying the detritus of decades into trash bags. I said only that I had been at the swimming pool.

"Don't move the furniture!" my father nearly shouted, his voice strong and clear, his eyes still closed.

Unlike Emily Brontë's Keeper, Libro was not part of the funeral ceremony. I took what I wanted of my parent's accumulated possessions, sold what I could, including the shiny Oldsmobile that had been my father's pride, shipped more, and brought Libro home.

∽

On a bright September morning two days after I'd returned from burying my father, two airplanes crashed into the World Trade Center. I'd walked two blocks to the elementary school where voting in the city primary election was taking place and talked with my neighbors waiting on line there about the increasingly perilous state of the union. On my way home, I crossed paths with a woman walking her dog who told me that a plane had hit a downtown building. I remembered flying in a twin-engine craft from upstate New York, following the course of the Hudson River all the way to the tip of Manhattan and circling the towers close enough to see the faces of people working inside. Oh dear, I thought, and I walked home a little faster.

Libro looked up at me as I crossed the living room to turn on the television. We were comfortable as old shoes by now, able to simply nod "hello" without much fuss. I sank to the couch. He climbed up beside me. Buildings fell, people jumped, people ran for their lives. Clouds of dust and smoke, choruses of tears and screams. A clip of the president, reading a story to schoolchildren. Car alarms howling on my street and dogs barking. The phone ringing and ringing again. Libro moving closer.

Late in the afternoon, I came to, having done nothing for hours but sit on the couch, stare at the screen, shiver, cry, and clutch Libro tightly in my arms. He had stayed tight against my trembling body, not even leaving me for a trip to his water bowl. I revived when I did, not because the horror was over—it was not— but because life intruded. Libro's heart was beating, his lungs were pumping and his kidneys were filling. He needed to pee, needed badly, mercifully, to get out.

I got his leash. We went down the stairs, he hurrying. The street had a funereal air. People looked at one another blankly. What could you say? Even the occasional dog seemed quiet and sad or frightened, except for Olga's dog Trixie, who was yapping wildly. We went to the corner and down into Riverside Park.

Libro peed, many times. We sat on the grass and looked at the sparkling river and the sturdy buildings on the New Jersey side while sirens roared up and down the shut-down West Side Highway, carrying help south to the World Trade Center and away from it.

Knots of people began to appear, walking north through the park, eyes straight ahead, not speaking to anyone in that eerie silence. Dust and ash covered their clothes and some of their faces. Survivors. Zombies. Phantasms. I put my arms around Libro again.

You're still here. I'm still here. We're still here.

Home again, we went out on the south-facing terrace, with its purple morning glories now shriveled in the shade, its tangerine and red roses still open, its herbs still vibrant. I could see smoke, miles away, and I could smell something I would later identify as death. Libro looked up at the sky and began to bark. On and on, he barked, furiously.

What to do? What to do? Hold tight to your friends. Hug your dog. What else?

As I began to recover the ability to think, the day after, what I did was go to the smoky tip of Manhattan, just to see, just to believe. I passed fences covered with photos of "lost" people and took flyers from the hands of many who had clearly not been to bed. Back home, I ran into the doctor on the street, returning from an emergency room stint. He told me this story:

The morning before the planes hit, a man who worked in the World Trade Center was getting ready to leave for his job, but his German shepherd blocked the doorway. This had never happened before. He told the dog to move. The dog lay down. The man grew insistent and still the dog would not move. Exasperated, he bent over to grab the collar. His dog bit him. At 9:04 in the morning, as the second plane slammed into the building, the man who worked in the World Trade Center was in the emergency room of Beekman Downtown Hospital, having his hand treated for a severe dog bite.

I went upstairs to find Libro pawing at the terrace door, frantic to get out.

Would he have saved me if I needed saving? Could he save me now? Neither I nor anyone I knew could begin to identify what being saved would look like. We were, like the rest of the country, still in shock, still in disbelief, but Libro corrected the disbelief. It had, his nose told him, even five miles north of ground zero, actually happened.

He was nearly ripping the door apart.

I let him outside, where the terrace garden was a riot of plenty, growing toward harvest time. Oregano spilled over its wooden box and purple morning glories were open on the peeling white wooden fence. The miniature red roses were picture perfect. But Libro only sat, staring south, inhaling the aroma of burning flesh and crumbled steel, and barking in full fury at the sky.

He would go on doing that for days. Friends said their dogs were trembling or hiding or refusing to go outside, but Libro was in a state of outrage, as he always was when the world was not behaving according to his code of civilized conduct.

In the weeks that followed, I donated blood and made many phone calls, including some to people still searching for abandoned animals downtown and others who were working with their animals to comfort the workers at the site and the survivors at centers that were springing up everywhere. I made lists and appointments to volunteer. Libro liked it much better when I got busy instead of sitting on the couch weeping and I believe he knew that he would be included in whatever I was planning.

You would think that a tragedy of this magnitude would stifle commerce, but getting and spending went on. In the midst of "recovery" taking place in our city, the book that took our story public was published in paperback. Because ours was a tale of rescue, because the coffers were running low and because life, we were all constantly being told, went on, it seemed a good thing to gear up for another round of appearances. Besides, I knew how much Libro enjoyed appearances.

At a pet store in Greenwich Village, almost within sight of the still smoldering ruins, Libro sat on the sidewalk one brisk fall Sunday afternoon as we, like old time pushcart peddlers, hawked our tome to passersby. While New Yorkers may not have been much interested in books during that time—it being difficult to sit quietly and read while your head is throbbing, your hands shaking and your eyes nervously scanning the sky—they were extremely interested in animals. The pet store owners had stacks of newly ordered supplies, including many carriers for small pups, which told me that downtown dwellers—I suspected they were uncoupled dwellers—were bringing into their lives companion animals that could companion them everywhere they went. Book sales were meager that day, but encounters of the amorous kind were numerous, with strangers stopping to pet and hug Libro, sometimes in crushing embraces. He seemed neither to know nor to mind that this affection had been prompted by heartbreak, horror and need.

This round of appearances brought us yet another airplane trip. By now, Libro was an expert in getting into his "little house" and I was an expert at assembling and disassembling the travel crate, getting us and it to the airport with a minimum of fuss. No tranquilizers any more for either of us.

The airport, however, was far from tranquil, so soon after 9/11. Armed National Guardsmen stood around in battle gear looking young and terrified. Local police eyed every car that pulled up in front of the terminal. Inside, travelers and friends eyed the police and each other with equal wariness. Libro's crate had not yet been set up for transport and he was on his leash, not the least bit wary, but friendly and excited, accompanying me on the check-in line where I would pay his fare.

Some fears must be greater than other fears because, unlike previously, Libro's appearance in the airport terminal was welcomed. No one shied away. "Oh, good," one woman in line said, smiling, "a bomb-sniffing dog."

And when Libro was safely in his crate, rolled away and placed in the hold, the plane lifted off, flying over Manhattan, heading south.

"Ladies and gentlemen," the captain said, as though he was pointing out the Grand Canyon, "below you on the left side of the aircraft, you can see Ground Zero."

I looked down at the scarred scene and wondered if Libro was barking furiously down there with the cargo.

Our destination was the Amelia Island Book Festival, off the coast of northern Florida. We arrived in

Jacksonville, Libro none the worse for the journey, and proceeded to the rental lot, where the only vehicle available was a silver Mustang convertible. Since the trunk space was too small for the travel crate, Libro had to ride beside me in the front seat. No Armani sunglasses.

*Eso es vivir*, all over again. Life did indeed go on.

Amelia Island and its historic town, Fernandina Beach, were charming. While other authors who had come for the book fair were housed in a rather standard hotel, Libro and I got to stay in a Victorian bed and breakfast inn, the only "dog friendly" accommodation on the island. This time, as honored guests, we were not relegated to any hotelier's version of a doghouse, but instead given a sunny room, trimmed with patchwork and calico, on the second floor, up a twisty flight of stairs. Libro loved the bed.

I began to realize how much we needed a vacation, and though he and I did one reading together, stamping copies of the book with that green-ink paw, and I spoke as part of a panel about memoir writing, there was plenty of free time and warm weather. But each time we set out for a relaxing walk, I was startled by a sharp pull on the leash and a lunging Libro. The island, known as a center for shrimp fishing on the eastern seaboard, was full of cats. And they weren't in hats—this was, after all, a gathering of book people. No, these were actual, live, feral cats, skulking along the streets, hiding under

porches and tempting Libro like hissing Scheherazades
or meowing mermaids come from the briny waters that
surrounded us. Though all his younger disruptive habits
had long since disappeared—he never jumped on
people with that old puppy enthusiasm and he usually
walked quietly at my side without yearning to be leader
of our pack—he still went for cats. I understood. To my
dying day, there will be things of the world that push
my buttons, too. Still, our leisure was hampered by the
omnipresence of prey.

Hogging the spotlight, here and elsewhere, often
compensated for other deprivations. We could not take
our ease in the streets, but we could be the festival's
door prize. A lucky winner drew a ticket for a beach
walk with Libro. Off we went on the last day, safely en-
closed in a car, to a beautiful white beach on the Atlantic Ocean. A lucky couple from Georgia disappeared
from sight, leaving four human and four canine foot-
prints in their wake. I was nervous and proud, but Libro
was in all his glory, not a feline to be seen and a knot of
admiring humans awaiting and applauding his return.

Back in New York, the National Guard still patrolled
the airport. Home was a trifle musty because I'd closed
the windows to keep out the dust from Ground Zero,
which may or may not have actually floated five miles
uptown. The blinking red light on my answering machine indicated many messages. Among them was an

opportunity to volunteer with Libro as a pet therapy team.

My decision to enroll in pet therapy training was not only a reaction to the attack on our city and part of the subsequent wave of civic-mindedness among its citizens, but a tardy acknowledgement of the fact that Libro was a natural healer. He had always been drawn to hurt people, pulling me toward wheelchairs or crutches or slow, tired walkers and placing himself beside them as guardian and comforter. His gimpy leg, I believed, endowed him with compassion for other wounded souls. To know that this was true, you had only to look into his deep amber eyes.

Also, not being one to rest on his laurels, nap the day away, or even to remain engrossed in my tapping at the computer keyboard, Libro, I knew, needed a job. But before he could have a job or even be eligible for job training, he had to audition.

In the past, I'd felt the need to coach Libro for public appearances where something—like book sales—was at stake. Sue the trainer, however, had assured me that all she wanted was to see the dog's temperament at their first meeting. I merely reiterated "be yourself," as though he could do otherwise, and walked Libro down to the west eighties.

We met Sue on the sidewalk outside her building. Libro was, indeed, himself. "Friendly" would be an understatement. Seductive and slobbery, more accurately, captivating Sue with his eyes, sitting when asked, lying down when requested, but most of all, demonstrating the capacity for calm relatedness necessary for therapy work. Sue pointed out his one bad habit: if you offered Libro a biscuit, he took it enthusiastically, in my version, but kind of dangerously, in Sue's. I'd never noticed or cared, but an experienced trainer like Sue believed we would need to work on that. It was important that the people Libro "served" feel free to proffer edibles without worrying about losing their fingers.

Perfection was not demanded. Libro passed.

# 6

## Doctor Libro
## Goes to Work

*The one predominant duty is to
find one's work and do it.*
—Charlotte Perkins Gilman

"We're starting school today," I said, picturing Libro with preppie cap and backpack.

It was a long walk across Central Park from our Upper West Side abode to the ASPCA building very far east, but the air was nippy and we made good time crunching across the leaf-strewn ground. Like most dogs, Libro was better in cooler weather than he was when the outdoor temperature went over eighty degrees. His flat boxer nose and thin coat made it harder for him to cool off on those days, resulting in much imbibing from the water bottle I always carried and many pathetic-looking rest stops lying prone under trees or on shaded sidewalks, which frustrated my benevolent intention of getting him out and back into the air conditioning as quickly as possible. For a smart dog, he sometimes behaved in ways I thought kind of dumb, but then I'd remember that his logic was not the same as mine.

September and October were good months; winter wasn't bad, except for the wet snow and ice. You always knew it was September in the park, not just because the green leaves on the street turned russet and gold, but because all the dogs dashed around as though they were on speed. Like his canine tribe, Libro ran faster and longer in the fall, was more interested in playing with other dogs and was reluctant to go home.

In tune with the rest of the world, we were beginning school in the fall. At the door of the ASPCA building, we passed three dogs leashed together and being taken for a walk by a teenaged boy. I knew right away that they were strays, taken in or given to the agency, on their way out for brief recreation with a volunteer. How did I know? Circumstances helped—it was, after all the ASPCA—but the dogs, clean, well-fed, healthy though they were, had an unloved aura about them that was palpable. I resisted pointing this out to Libro as an object lesson about how lucky he was—there but for the grace of God go you—because by then I'd fully understood that I was the lucky one.

The large room on the second floor looked like an elementary-school lunchroom. Sue was arranging chairs in a circle and water bowls around the room. We were not the first students to arrive. A large female boxer stood in the corner, tightly held on a leash by a young white man with a woman beside him who might have been his sister or his wife.

Oh, good, I thought: a potential friend, maybe a school crush. I was still thinking this way, in spite of being shown that I could not manage Libro's social life no matter how hard I tried. He managed his own, creating friends or a pack according to desires I could not fathom, playing with dogs that I considered too large or small or old or young and turning his nose away from some I would have thought were a perfect match.

As Libro and I, with equal curiosity, approached, the large female boxer bared her teeth and growled. Her "people" told her to sit, but she kept growling and reared up like a mountain lion with her eyes fixed on Libro. We moved away.

Libro didn't seem to mind, quickly shifting his focus to Sue. When he was younger, he was more easily hurt, looking at me questioningly if a dog didn't respond to him or menaced him and, far too often for my peace of mind, trying over and over to win their attention if not their hearts. Now he gravitated toward dogs he had known for years. New arrivals—transplants from places like Ohio or month-old puppies—were checked out but not engaged.

Like most old married couples, neither Libro nor I at this point cared much for making new conquests, especially if they seemed difficult from the start. I knew we were getting older because what once promised excitement—a romp with a new creature—now seemed like too much trouble. I'd barely thought about conquests of the human kind since I'd discovered that the man with a dachshund was nice to his dog but not to me. I couldn't tell if I was just licking my wounds, if I'd given up on the Adam and Eve business forever, or if I'd simply made a choice for what was becoming a very long moment. The sexy French actor Brigitte Bardot once said that she had given the first part of her life to men and was going to give the second part of her life to animals, but I would hardly go that far. I wasn't interested in animals, plural.

For better or for worse, though I couldn't begin to imagine "worse," Libro and I were clearly stuck with each other.

Class began. The people sat on the chairs, dogs at their feet. Sue, dressed in sweats, her dark hair in a ponytail, stood in the middle of the room. Libro fixated his eyes and his nose on Sue, not because he was the perfect student, but because she had treats in her pocket. He paid no attention to the tiny Yorkie in a red sweater, the sweet female golden retriever, or the huge, docile black-and-white dog of mixed ancestry who had joined the class, or to the girl boxer, still held in a corner away from the others, or to me. None of the other dogs behaved this way, but then none of the other dogs had Libro's history and none of them lived with me.

Libro had arrived in my life already having learned most of the things we expect dogs who live with people to know. His actual comprehension by now, I believed, extended to several hundred words, including "I'm working" and "we're going home" and "what do you think?" The only behavioral adjustments I'd attempted were to teach him not to jump on people and to remind him to walk beside me instead of acting like the lead sled dog in the Iditarod. He had never been bribed with treats. I, the daughter of a man who owned a candy store, a girl with fillings in all her teeth by the time she was twelve, an obsessive exerciser and recovering fat-phobic, did not believe in treats, for myself or for my dog. Therefore, I reasoned, if Sue had edibles in her pockets, it would never occur to Libro that he had to do something to get them.

The first half-hour was meant to remove any fear of strangers that the dogs might have and accustom them to being touched by people they didn't know. We aced that one. Libro had been patted and pawed all the way from Florida to the California coast. Like me, his idea of hell was being ignored. Fear of strangers? This was a dog who spied strangers on Broadway walking with cameras dangling from their necks and placed himself squarely in their path, ready for his close-up. This guy ran to a crowd in our neighborhood that was shooting a segment of the TV show *Law and Order*, not only making sure he was noticed, but finding his way to the show's star, Jerry Orbach, sitting in a canvas chair, and climbing up into his lap.

Next came some training about remaining calm while peculiar objects were moved around the room. Sue and her assistant clanked and banged hospital walkers, IV stands, and wheelchairs back and forth. Sue gave an especially good performance as a feeble old lady pushing her walker and then as a trembling patient in a wheelchair. The Maltese yapped at her. Libro, resting on his paws, didn't even turn his head. He lived on the Upper West Side of Manhattan! He had seen peacocks fan their tails. He had been in planes, trains, automobiles, and sailboats. He had ridden in the laps of people in wheelchairs on the street. At least one of the people he knew used a scooter because polio was stiffening her legs and he always walked serenely beside it unless offered a ride, which he eagerly accepted. He had witnessed half-dead zombies stumbling in Riverside Park after the 9/11 attacks and a man on a bench with his sleeve rolled up and a hypodermic in his hand, ready to shoot up, saying directly into Libro's eyes, "I'm sorry you have to see this."

Sue dismissed us, instructing us to practice our new tasks during the week and to study our dogs for signs of stress. Stress? Boredom was more like it, since the first lesson had been so easy for Libro. When I was in school, boredom led to discipline problems and I hoped that wasn't going to happen now.

The only man in the class offered us a ride back across Central Park. His name was Larry, he lived in Westchester County, just north of the West Side, and he drove a new black Lexus. Larry and his retriever took the front seat; Libro and I collapsed in the back.

I had some opinions about the training session, which was natural, since I had always had trouble with authority, but especially with one-size-fits-all standard curricula. You'd think I was back in college, arguing about needing to learn geology or in graduate school, complaining about all the dead white males I was forced to read. Larry, being a live white male, was not as critical as I was, nor very interested in having an engaging conversation with me. He spent most of the ride home petting his dog and telling her how good she had been.

Second class was a week later. The lesson was rolling over. Just as I didn't "believe" in endless treats, my enormous respect for Libro had led me to see silly tricks as violations of his dignity. He had never been asked to roll over or to beg, which would hurt his back legs, and certainly not to "speak," since he did so eloquently with his eyes. Other dogs in the room lived with humans who believed otherwise. They rolled over without complaint or difficulty and got treats for doing so. The Maltese, this time in a green sweater, kept rolling over and over and over.

I had to help Libro accomplish this task, holding his paws, as Sue instructed, and virtually turning him onto his back, then onto his belly again, cooing "good dog" and sticking a treat in his mouth. He did it all awkwardly, letting us know he didn't get the point. Not a robot. Thinking for himself was, to me, the sign of a good dog, but the goal, I reminded myself, was service. We would go forth from this training to be helpful in the world, which could use all the help it could get. It would make life easier if I stopped having opinions.

Most of my opinions, though, were about Libro, me and healing, which I'd had some experience with. We were who we were, Libro and I, a dog of a certain age—he was now going on six—and a woman of a certain age. We were smart. We were compassionate, he more than I, and sensitive and responsive to others. But we were also quite set in our ways, teachable, perhaps, but not in line for major personality transformations. One of the great joys for me of turning fifty had been to recognize this. If Libro would not drink out of the water bowl in the classroom because others had been there before him, that was fine with me. Next time, I'd bring his bowl. What had standardized good behavior to do with the idiosyncrasies of love, comfort, and healing?

Larry gave us another ride home and showed me the book he had written about his gay marriage.

The third class involved more tricks, including learning to "give paw." Sideshow stuff. Memories of myself as a child model—pushed and shoved, arranged and rearranged—surfaced, but I tried anyway—following Sue's instructions to hold the treat behind Libro's shoulder, which made him twist to get it and brought one paw off the ground. I gave the treat. Good paw. I still had opinions. I hated this. Libro would be a good therapist without having to turn himself into a sword swallower.

There were three more sessions. Learning to take treats nicely from someone's hand remained a sticking point for Libro. He still hoovered a bit, but he didn't bite, which was, presumably, the main danger. I couldn't help but picture a disconcerting scene in which a little old lady in a pink lace-trimmed bed jacket welcomes Libro only to find him pawing through the gumdrops

on her bedside table. She reaches a trembling hand out
to pet him. *Whoosh!* Gone are the gum drops and her
ring finger. Stubbornly rebellious, still proud of who Libro was in his heart and in his soul, I was in need of my
own attitude correction. In spite of myself, I wanted
him to be the best in the class. I had to bite my tongue
to keep from letting him know that. Luckily, there
were no grades. The girl boxer dropped out and the rest
of the class passed. At graduation, Libro got a blue bandana, a symbol of his official status as a therapy dog. He
allowed Sue to tie the symbol around his neck. She
gave him a treat. Larry and his dog did not show up.

Before our first excursion as a therapy team, to a Christmas party for "underprivileged" children, I cleaned Libro's ears (he made an awful face) and brushed his
teeth (then he made a face beyond awful). Just adher-
ing to protocol, I apologized. But sometimes, I warned
him, rebellion is counterproductive and you just have
to go along to get along. After a long walk in the park
to tire him out, I tied the blue bandana around his
neck, and Doctor Libro was ready for work. He knew,
of course, that something was up, something good, but
apparently not a beach trip because he had a blue bandana instead of a packed green-and-white tote bag.
Leashless, he raced down the stairs, out the front door,
into the waiting car, sitting primly, eagerly, even impa-
tiently on the back seat.

We drove through heavy traffic to midtown and stopped in front of a tall office building. In the lobby, we were directed to the public elevators. In what was clearly not dog territory, Libro's presence usually called for special vertical transportation, namely the freight elevator, though he had once ridden with the crowds in the Condé Nast building, wearing his "Visitor" tag. We rode the elevator this time along with some people in business suits, all of whom appeared agreeably surprised by the unexpected sight of a dog with a bright blue bandana around his neck, as though a single flower had popped up in vibrant glory on a concrete sidewalk. Libro paid them no mind, fascinated as he was by whatever his nose told him as he pressed it against the doors. Presumably something indicated we were standing still and moving at the same time, a condition more difficult to explain than peacocks on a lawn or deer on a country road.

In what I'd been told was corporately donated office space, kids of various ages were sitting around a large table noisily doing crafts, laughing, screaming, and throwing bits of clay at each other, under the supervision of a few adults. At the sight of Libro coming through the door, some raced over, dropping to the floor to embrace him. He took it well, though I worried about suffocation. One girl, her hair in beautifully beaded cornrows, hanging back, asked, "Does he bite?"

My wise-ass answer, "only if you bite him," was not appropriate in this situation, so I simply said, reassuringly, "no." The girl still hung back.

"Would you like to give the dog a biscuit?" I said, mindful of my lessons in training class.

The girl took a step away, but a brave boy put out his hand.

I took the biscuit from my purse. Libro tried to eat it with his eyes, but I passed it to the boy and told Libro to sit. The moment of truth had arrived.

"Gently, gently," I said to Libro. *Don't bite the kid's hand off*, I thought. He didn't, but he did want more biscuits, of course.

By then, two boys around five and seven years old were playing with him. When I heard them speak to each other in Spanish, I told Libro to *siéntate*, which he willingly did.

"*¿El perro habla español?*"

"*Si.*"

The boys could not believe it. They should only know that he speaks Korean, too, I thought, but a quick survey of the room revealed no Asian children and so I did not mention it.

"*Levántate*," I said and Libro stood up.

The older boy tried it.

"*Siéntate*," he commanded. Libro sat.

"*Levántate*," he said, like a drill sergeant. Libro got up.

They called their friends over. "*Oye, Carlos, el perro habla español!*" one of them shouted over the din and Carlos came running, accompanied by half a dozen friends.

"*Siéntate! Levántate.*" And sit and get up, on and on, a willing but increasingly weary Libro looking toward me—how long do I have to be a good dog?

As our life together had gone on, I had found myself giving Libro fewer and fewer instructions because he generally knew what to do and a look would often suffice because we understood each other without words. I almost never had to make decisions for him either. I was struggling, then, with whether or not I should intervene on Libro's behalf as he did what amounted to gymnastic squats over and over. When the children tried to feed him gobs of clay, I stepped in.

Just as the words "no" and "stop" came out of my mouth, a woman came and asked if we might not want a little quiet. Although she appeared as an angelic savior, she was actually a volunteer with the charity giving the party, and the room she led us into, after Libro had gulped three bowls of water, had a massage table.

Libro was panting hard, from excitement, exhaustion, or the overheated room. We moved a chair closer to the massage table so he could climb onto it. It took a very long time for Libro to lie down—he turned in circles—tearing the thin paper that covered the table, but when he did, the woman placed her hands gently on his body and he sighed. As he grew quiet, she moved those hands around, up and down, fluttering them above his body. Fluffing his aura, she said.

And why not? Libro had a book agent, a publisher, an accountant, a banker, several dog nannies, an acupuncturist, and a spiritual advisor. Why not an aura-fluffer?

He did look refreshed, but I'd had enough. As we passed through the main room again on our way out, the boys and their friend Carlos came running after us, shouting "Libro! Libro!" but we escaped into the hallway. The body worker accompanied us to the elevators and said she had something to tell me. I was afraid she wanted to ask us to come back for another therapy session. She leaned toward me and whispered, so Libro could not, she believed, hear.

"His brain area was very, very warm," she said. "I could feel the activity there in my hands. He thinks triple time. He thinks he is smarter than you are and that he has to watch out for both of you."

The elevator came just in time.

On the busy street, I tried to hail a cab, which is not easy in midtown under the best of circumstances and doubly difficult when you have a large dark canine in tow. But the blue bandana was a piece of magic and a cab did eventually pull up. The driver, bearded and turbaned, lowered his window and I explained that the dog was a therapy dog and had been hard at work, so we were allowed in.

Libro crawled onto my lap and closed his eyes. The driver watched us in his rear view window. Since my aura had not been fluffed, and I, too, needed body work, my thoughts were not the sanest: Whaddya mean, you think you're smarter than I am? Of course, I know my smeller doesn't work 1/100th as well as yours, but. . . .

Libro did not lift his head until we were home. Zonked. We both needed an hour of meditation. I ate a huge dinner and went to bed early. He'd been asleep for hours.

In my opinion, the place had been too noisy, too crowded, not a lot of fun for Libro and not what I had in mind. We needed quieter, more intimate situations and opportunities for healing more profound than being a plaything. The next time Sue asked us to visit the children, I had the flu and the time after that, friends were in town.

From Christmas to Easter, Libro's requirement for care increased. He had never been a perfect physical specimen. But his turned-out back leg and achy hips had been worsening over time in spite of acupuncture and massage. On an x-ray, his hipbones looked so eroded that they reminded me of the stark bone and dry desert of some Georgia O'Keefe paintings. If he was in pain though, he had hidden it, which dogs do, to avoid becoming prey to stronger animals. I imagined that because he thought he was smarter than I, he was determined to be my strong and vigilant protector, no matter what.

Remedies ranging from plant extracts to chemical concoctions were recommended for joint pain. Our morning and evening rituals—one capsule for him, one for me—took longer and longer. He moved ahead of me in terms of volume. The medication for arthritis required monitoring of his blood for possible liver damage, so we went to the vet with increasing frequency, which pleased Libro no end.

I surprised myself. Given the devil-may-care free-for-all that my life had been before Libro sneaked into it, it was hard to believe how little resentment I felt about the inconvenience he could be. I had walked him every day, even when the thermometer dipped below thirty and the wind off the Hudson River lacerated my skin or when it climbed beyond ninety and I could not catch a breath. Voyages in inclement weather had turned out to be adventures at best, shared discomfort at worst.

Even more surprising was my ability to cope with debility or illness. It was not in my genes. Counterphobic would likely sum up my attitude. Coming as I did from a family of hysterics, hypochondriacs, and drama queens, not to mention people with serious illnesses, I'd resisted turning myself into Florence Nightingale and become, instead, a fanatically independent, self-reliant Wonder Woman in this regard. Worse than a dog, who felt pain even when he did not let on, I convinced myself of strength, health, and invincibility. I'd refused the ambulance a friend offered after my surgery. Until Libro showed me a different way, I'd been Hard Hearted Hannah around illness, hospitals, doctors, and medicine, a trait for which I continually apologized to people I loved.

For the new me, this ministering to him was a no-brainer.

By the spring, he seemed vaguely worse. All I could say was that he didn't seem quite himself. What did that mean? Mothers know. Others think "not himself" is a nutty description of a dog, but he felt different to me in ways more troublesome than what a fluffed aura might repair. His muzzle had been getting grayer, which I took to be merely a sign of aging and I had even joked about using my own hair coloring on him because the match was so close. But, far less humorously, he had been drinking a lot more water, emptying the bowl and asking for more, then needing to go outside more often. His maple fudge coat seemed duller and thinner. He walked more slowly and lay down on the sidewalk with increasing frequency, even though the weather was temperate. But he still went up and down the stairs effortlessly, and when he got to the park, he ran without limping or stopping, using his heavily muscled chest to propel him, the weaker rear part of his body just following along like a train's caboose. If only we could keep running and never have to stop.

"Are you okay?"

No answer, though his eyes looked as lively and profound as ever.

"You want to go see Doctor K.?"

Boy, did he. He pulled me toward the doctor's office as though we were headed for the pet store, his second favorite establishment. When I didn't open the office door quickly enough, he pawed at it, dashing past the other patients, most of whom were cowering and trembling with fear. Libro went straight to the receptionist's desk and was given a biscuit. Or five biscuits. Then he tried to cut the line of waiting people and dogs and cats, heading straight toward the examining rooms. Restrained from doing so, he lay across the hallway leading to those rooms, blocking the passage.

His enthusiasm for his doctor, the vet office, the biscuits, and the solicitous care would never wane over the months to come, no matter what procedures were inflicted on him. There were many procedures, beginning the following week with a test that required drawing blood at intervals throughout the day. Libro disappeared behind closed doors into the laboratory and operating room and emerged some minutes later looking none the worse for being pricked. He got biscuits and treats. We went home, where I tried to work, and then we returned for more pricking. We left, walked in the park, returned again and then I waited for results.

Elevated liver enzymes, Dr. K. said. Cushing's disease. Common in middle aged to older dogs. Symptoms are excessive drinking and urinating, increased appetite, thinning coat, and bloated belly. Caused by an excessive production of the adrenal hormone cortisol which, in turn, is due to a tumor on either the pituitary or adrenal gland.

A tumor.

Did tumor mean death?

A week later, after days of reminding myself to breathe, trying to focus on creating words and humming myself to sleep at night, while noticing that Libro apparently shared none of my fear, I learned that the tumor did not mean death and that, with medication, he would be "functional" for some time to come. My fingers fled to the Internet, where I saw pictures of dogs with advanced Cushing's disease that reminded me of concentration camp victims, and where I chatted online with others facing the same situation, no small comfort.

The medication that would slow down production of the hormone making him sick was added to the bottles on the kitchen countertop and after some weeks of tweaking the dosage, checking his blood levels each time, he improved. To my mind, Libro had beaten all the odds throughout his life and would do so again.

Within a year, Libro was better, according to lab tests and to me. Since he was obviously bored hanging out with me with nothing to do, I began investigating better places for him to resume his career as Doctor Libro. A psychiatric hospital in northern Manhattan was eager to experiment with pet therapy for comfort, perhaps even improvement for people suffering from intractable conditions like depression or even dementia. Personally, this appealed to me because I was beginning to think of myself as halfway between the depression of my early adulthood and the dementia I feared lurking in my twilight years.

Libro was as excited as ever riding uptown in a car and walking into a place with new people and new smells. Showing a marked preference for office secretaries over doctors and administrators, he wandered around licking people's hands. An administrator (male), doctor (male) and a social worker (female) interviewed us, sitting around a conference table, which reminded me of taking my oral exams in graduate school, but nobody asked questions about John Milton or Renaissance love poetry that I couldn't answer.

Libro sat on the floor looking compassionate and interested. You would never know that he was sick.

Whatever kind of audition the meeting was, I passed—they had paid little attention to Libro beyond admiring him—and we all moved on in a group across a cheerful atrium toward elevators that would take us, I believed, face to face with depression and dementia. But Libro kept looking at me with a familiar expression and shifting his eyes toward the lobby windows, so I asked for time out while we went outside. He drank a lot from the water bottle and I noticed thinning patches in his coat that I hadn't seen before.

We rejoined the others and ascended. In a large empty, sun-flooded room, the chairs were arranged in a circle, set up, they said, for group therapy sessions. This was where Libro would come weekly to work. He walked around, sniffing the floor while the people sat on some of the chairs and the social worker wrote on her yellow legal pad. The doctor and the administrator checked their beepers frequently while we all chatted. Libro came back and lay at my feet, panting heavily. Or collapsed at my feet, which is what it looked like to me. I got down on the floor, still chatting, cradling him and then rubbing his back gently. He stood up, shook his body, clanking the rabies and ID tags he wore on his collar and gave my face a long, grateful licking.

That was a mistake. Not on Libro's part—he was just being a dog—but on mine, as I was told the next day. We were rejected by the hospital because our "behavior violated the boundaries" and would make patients uncomfortable. Dogs, in the world of boundaries, stayed on the floor; people stayed on the chairs. And n'er the twain shall meet. Nor kiss. Actually, given the little I know about having your mental processes acting like a washing machine on spin cycle, the objection made professional sense. In truth, though, given a choice between siding with professional sense and siding with Libro, I believed I'd made the right choice and that we needed to continue looking for a suitable place.

I found a better opportunity at a large hospital complex uptown that was recruiting therapy teams for its pediatric cancer ward. A thorough physical exam for me; a certificate of health for Libro and a three-day training session brought us into July. The bald spots on his coat had begun to fade, but I was concerned about Libro's stamina on hot days. Two weeks later, we went uptown in an air-conditioned cab to be photographed for identification cards. As we walked through the hospital corridors, the sight of Libro trotting along evoked smiles on the faces of people in white coats. A clerk in the business office took my picture, using a camera exactly like the one at the Motor Vehicle Bureau. I had slim hopes for a flattering photo. Then, together, the clerk and I hoisted Libro onto a countertop for his. Accustomed to top-of-the-line photographers who came with multiple cameras and assistants, he just sat quietly while the office worker snapped away.

The lights went out the next day. Actually, there were few lights on that August afternoon, so I noticed the lack of air conditioning first. It had been running full-blast and Libro, as usual, had been lying on the floor right in front of it. I was working at my desk when I began to feel a little warm. I checked the machine, which was dead. Libro hadn't moved, but he did look up expectantly as I fiddled with the knobs, unplugged the line, plugged it in again and cursed the rising costs of my wonderful life, which would now apparently include a new air-conditioning unit.

The radio didn't work, nor the TV, nor the lights. Like everyone else, I thought it might be another terrorist attack. I tried to call Olga, but the phone was dead, too. Dragging Libro on his leash—he seemed to think that remaining near the air conditioner, working or not, would keep him cool—we went downstairs. Olga wasn't home, but Trixie was yapping plaintively behind the locked door. Libro barked back at her. I warned him about heat exhaustion. Out in the street, a man parking his car told us he'd heard on his radio that the city was experiencing a power blackout. I had lived through two blackouts before, but not with a dog.

We stayed outside for hours, joining local people congregating in Straus Park, where we had last been assembled for an antiwar vigil. We sat in a circle around a battery-operated radio, tracking the blackout up and down the East Coast, while police sirens wailed up and down Broadway. It was nearing five—Libro's dinnertime—when we went home to find the hallway dark and the staircase even darker. This mattered not a whit to Libro, who "saw" with his nose.

"Go up," I said. And he did, with me behind him, navigating toward home by the feel of my hand on his rump. Now I knew how safe and located blind people feel when their fingers touch their canes or a page of Braille.

We were, in fact, safe, though it was very hot. Libro had dry food for supper and I ate some yogurts from the warming refrigerator. I poured bottled water onto a washcloth and cooled Libro down every half-hour. The hardest part was having nothing to do, realizing how reliant I was on electric light to read by or the television set or the sound system. My respect for our ancestors increased when I tried to read by candlelight only to find that even a dozen candles barely illuminated the page. There was nothing to do but go to sleep, Libro and I, sweating and tossing side by side. We got power back the next day.

One year later, it was the kind of late summer evening that people who live outside New York City don't believe we have. The humidity was low. You could smell fall in the air. Everything was fresh and had sharp, clearly defined edges.

Mr. Wexler, as his wife Pamela called him, sweated up four flights of stairs, to be met in the apartment doorway by Libro, who had been anticipating visitors from the moment I'd cleared the floor of his toys and set the outdoor table. This time, he was right.

Pamela was familiar, he'd met her many times, but the big human guy had to undergo extended nasal scrutiny. Somewhere around him there was the smell of cat—hated cat!—but Libro was a polite host, and even though he emitted a brief snarl as he ran his nose over Mr. Wexler's trouser cuffs, they were allowed to stay.

Chicken marinated in lime juice cooked on the grill in my outdoor garden in the sky. Our conversation avoided politics because the peculiar thing about Barry Wexler, a smart, witty and aware fellow, was that he seriously listened to Rush Limbaugh, and he really trusted those folks in the White House. To this pinko feminazi, to use Limbaugh's so-called vocabulary, Wexler seemed far to the right of Attila the Hun. But Libro, who had done voter registration wearing a sign that said, "I pee on bushes," was tolerant of Wexler's views and so, knowing all Barry's redeeming qualities, I followed suit.

Soon after sunset, Pamela with her guy and I with mine, we went to Riverside Park for an outdoor show-ing of *On the Waterfront*, with the Hudson River as backdrop. With sweaters over our shoulders and satis-fied stomachs, we settled happily onto a hilly slope packed with picnickers, blankets, neighbors and the occasional dog. Rod Steiger. Marlon the hunk. Eva Marie, the saint. By the time the thugs were pursuing Brando, Libro's bladder was reacting to the many bowls of water imbibed on this warm night. Pamela and I were riveted to the screen. Barry, obviously not a man made for sprawling on beach blankets in the scratchy grass and perhaps also not made for Elia Kazan's vision of labor struggles and working class he-roes, was a little restless. So Barry picked up Libro's leather leash and took him off for a walk.

Libro had been abandoned in that very park years before by persons unknown and so was saddled with what shrinks call dependency issues. Although he was agreeable, even fond, of people who were not me, he never willingly disappeared from my view. But when Barry picked up the leash, Libro rose as though a walk with the big guy was the most natural thing in the world and off they went together, while the silver screen flickered. Wexler seemed a little self-conscious. Libro didn't look back.

Apparently having experienced that mysterious state called male bonding, neither Barry nor Libro reported what conversations and what adventures they had on their junket. As they returned, I looked at my beautiful dog, in the flickering light of the movie screen, taking in the spreading gray on his face that made him appear more pale than old and the fading color of his coat, which, in that light, was the color of salt. A chill went through me.

7

# Dreaming in Libro

*I think that the dying pray at the last not "please," but "thank you," as a guest thanks his host at the door.*
—Annie Dillard

Libro's ninth "birthday," as I had designated Memorial Day, found us alone together in the city because it would have been hard to travel with a dog who was not quite up to par. I actually like spending holiday weekends in town, when there are seats at the movies, tables in restaurants, and breathing space everywhere, but this time I only wanted to be home with Libro. When walking tired him, as it did more frequently, I lay down on the sidewalk right beside him and told him it was okay, that he could take as long as he liked before moving on. It actually was cooler there. Most pedestrians smiled and walked around us. A few said that their dogs lay down on the sidewalk a lot, too. People I didn't know asked what was wrong with him and how old he was.

The dog people in the run, where Libro no longer wished to do anything but sit on my lap on the bench, offered advice. While no one suggested voodoo rituals, which I half-expected, given the character of our district, prayer was certainly mentioned. On Memorial Day weekend and throughout the coming summer months, I was given the names of many animal doctors, including specialists, some as far away as California. It reminded me of the days before abortion was legal and everyone had a name and a phone number to pass on, usually beginning with, "I know a guy in . . ." I heard about many alternative healers and many kinds of potions. As I had done when I researched my options after a cancer diagnosis, I took to carrying a notebook at all times to record the information. I heard miracle stories about dogs at death's doorstep who lived for years after ingesting various extracts. I believed them all.

From his normal weight of sixty-five pounds, Libro was down to fifty-four by the middle of June. A bare patch that had appeared on his leg was biopsied by his vet, and blood was drawn for further investigation of what was wrong. Powders and pills to boost his immune system were prescribed. The doormen along Riverside Drive doled out extra biscuits; the Korean grocer promised a prayer in her temple; and Eddie the mailman simply shook his head helplessly.

Libro didn't seem to know he was sick. He ate voraciously, wolfing down the food in his bowl and begging for more, which I gave him. Although I knew that increased appetite was a sign of Cushing's disease, the atavistic Jewish mother that I never knew I had inside me took his relish for food as a good thing, a sign of health. As the temperature rose, he lay, as always, directly in front of the blasting air conditioner, inhaling it. Late afternoons on the terrace, he followed every buzzing insect with the menacing focus of a born hunter, daring them to come to rest anywhere near him or me. He was as interested as ever in Ben's poker game, as jealous as ever of Trixie occupying Olga's affections, as eager as ever to unravel the mysteries of a rawhide bone and as comfortable as ever tucking himself against me for an evening of homebound entertainment, books, television, or talking on the phone.

When the hospital called to arrange Doctor Libro's first visit to real live patients, I said we had better wait until the weather was a little cooler.

Summer all over the country meant not just dogs collapsed in front of air conditioners, humans battling ticks in the great outdoors, and tedious reruns on television, but, for a small minority, opportunities for writers to emerge from the solitude of their working lives and commune with those who aspired to be just like them. From Maine to California, writing workshops and conferences drew hungering folks whose idea of heaven was not big-time, lucrative screenplays or miniseries, but the more old fashioned forms of fiction, poetry, and drama, bless their souls. And memoir, the literary flavor of the month. I was invited to teach a weeklong intensive workshop in memoir writing and naturally, Libro was invited, too.

The campus was under an hour's drive, north of the city. I got lost the first day, worrying about Libro panting away in the back seat, taking the wrong fork in the road and heading toward the Catskill Mountains. Late, breathless and apologetic, I was greeted by a scowling session director, whose scowl faded when she laid eyes on Libro. The director's two dachshunds were waiting for us, too, sitting calmly at her feet. Once he had been given a large bowl of water, and in spite of the biological turmoil brewing in his body, Libro—who was quite fond of dachshunds—added a stern director, two dogs, and a dozen aspiring writers to his pack. He circled the seminar table where the class waited just as he had circled Ben's poker table, only this time, instead of chips and playing cards, he found scribbled-on manuscripts to sniff. This pleased him.

For a week, I worked with the red-faced man who had tracked down his biological parents, the eighty-year-old woman who had been a doctor's wife for sixty years, the former prison inmate and the other nine people of various ages with good stories to tell. Libro rested on the floor. From time to time, he trotted over to visit those at the table who welcomed him. If someone was reading to us from an especially difficult, emotional piece of writing, Libro would pay close attention, sitting very still on the floor, eyes wide and riveted on the person reading. After class, we retired to a stone cottage on the campus where I held individual conferences with each participant while Libro wandered in and out. I began to think that work might heal him.

On the last day, the writing faculty gave a reading. I stood at the lectern; Libro lay at my feet, facing the audience, which filled all the folding chairs and lined the back wall of an elegant, wood-paneled parlor room. It had been quite a few years since we did this particular "show," but he remembered the routine. When I was done and the audience applauded, he stood, tail wagging, but this time, he turned and faced me. Our eye contact was magnetic, but I remembered the television director's prohibition about offensive nether parts facing the audience and I wanted Libro to see all the people applauding him. He refused to turn around and continued to stare deep into my eyes with one of the very few expressions I had ever seen on his face that I could not fathom.

In early August, the vet's scale read fifty pounds. Dr. K. scheduled an ultrasound test and suggested a fatten-Libro-up diet of tonics and carbohydrates.

I cooked fettuccini and sprinkled it with olive oil. Libro hated the olive oil, I suppose, because he would take a mouthful of fettuccini and then, strands dripping from his dark muzzle, creating a hilarious chiaroscuro, wander around the kitchen shaking the pasta, flicking oil onto the walls, where it landed in patterns that reminded me of Jackson Pollock's paintings.

"He looks better. He's gained some weight, don't you think?" I said, a week later. The receptionist said yes, but the scale had gone from fifty to forty-five.

I began weighing him daily, even though I feared that I might have Munchausen syndrome, dragging the poor dog to the vet for warped reasons of my own. But science is science and the tests had shown what Dr. K. called a "mass" in his belly, a "mass" situated in a way that made it impossible to remove. I rubbed his belly but could feel nothing. I smelled it, sniffing for the mass, but there was no aura.

I had a choice to make. Unaccustomed as I was to making healthcare decisions for anyone, including myself, I had to decide whether or not to continue with medical procedures, which have, in the modern world, become nearly as sophisticated for animals as they are for humans. The "mass" could be biopsied, which would mean anesthesia and surgery. If it was cancerous, we could think about chemotherapy. My father had been able to make his wishes known—"do not resuscitate," he had said and signed. Aside from the way in which I believed I understood him, Libro could not really tell me how much he could take.

The crossroads was clear. Why do a biopsy if I was unwilling to act on the information it would provide, namely chemotherapy? Was he suffering or was he still a happy dog? I looked at Libro still flinging olive oil at the walls, still apparently chipper, not apparently in any pain. I decided: more pasta, no chemo.

This is the part they don't tell you about when you bring home a leaping, slobbering uncoordinated puppy. I spent all my time at home with Libro in a sweet haze, inhaling his scent, playing with his ears, holding him in my arms while at the same time, I talked with people who had "put their dogs to sleep," though the words barely came out of my mouth. "You killed him, you mean," I wanted to shout.

Heather told me how homeopathic remedies had kept Boo, the Dalmatian she had raised since he was five weeks old, alive for months, sick with kidney disease in his ninth year. When it came time to "put him to sleep," she held him in her arms, lying on the couch with her cat, who was his best friend, while a vet gave him a shot. She had already dug Boo's grave beneath a blue hydrangea in the yard and she buried him there wrapped in a flannel sheet. The cats refused to move away from the grave. Libro would have hated that story.

I'd had closer glimpses of the grief that comes with this inevitable stage of a dog's life. The answer, I knew, to "how long do they live?" is "not as long as we do." On one of our weighing-in visits to the vet, I'd seen a woman who lived with two white bulldogs, well known in the neighborhood, especially at Halloween, when the male appeared in a top hat and bib, the female in a tutu. But the female had been failing and the woman had been pulling the dog around the streets in a shiny red wagon. That day, the woman was weeping in the waiting room. Libro and I walked her home with the empty red wagon.

"Euthanasia," Dr. K. said, a gentle death, an act of mercy, but he was quick to add that Libro and I were not there yet, that I would know when the time came. How would I know?

"Are you done with this mortal coil, Libro?"
   "Are you finished?"
   "Are you ready to go?"
   Was I prepared to accept the answer?

My father had set the best example, not shirking the question and answering in the affirmative. At the end, he no longer worried about who would take care of me if I did not have a husband. That his mind was at ease about the daughter whose life had not taken the turns he would have wished for her I attributed to seeing me settled, calm, and happy. I owed much of that to Libro.

Libro had been my teacher for eight years, and I knew he would not falter now. If acceptance of change and loss is the lesson of most profound philosophies, Libro was still ready to teach and still smarter than I was, but he was not ready to go. He said *no* simply by shining his amber eyes back at me, tunnels to something I could not name, perhaps his soul. That look was intensely bright and steady, like a flame.

Barefoot and nightgown-clad at two in the morning with a brown boy uncontrollably peeing and too proud to have accidents in his home, I did feel like Libro's mommy. Mine was the panic known to single moms with sick children. When the scale dropped toward forty pounds and puddles of piss appeared on the floor indoors and more olive oil clung in layers on the walls, I leaned more heavily on the friends who had stepped forward when I had cancer and the new friends who were in my life because of Libro.

"I can't take this anymore," I wrote in e-mails. "I'm going crazy," I said on the phone.

"Hang on," e-mailed Doctor K. "Hang on," said Heather, on the phone.

I was coming to think of those two friends as the figures in old Matthew Brady photographs of the Civil War, the two soldiers who support and drag a wounded comrade off the battlefield.

I called the woman who owned the little red wagon and asked to borrow it. "I'm going to get you something to help you get around in the streets," I told Libro.

The wagon was in her hallway closet, disassembled for storage. We laid the pieces—wheels, axles, nuts, bolts, handles—on the floor and stared blankly at each other. She took from the closet a tool case as organized as anything I have ever seen, wrenches hung in order of ascending size, a dozen kinds of screwdrivers. I felt, to say the least, technologically challenged. I felt like a girl. I am the person who long ago would be setting up her computer, and when the words "run from DOS" appeared on the screen, I nearly raced to the other side of the room. When a bulb in a lamp goes out, I have been known to replace it, see that the new bulb does not work, get another and even check the fuse box before I realize that the lamp has come unplugged. Although there was a husband connected to the tool chest, we agreed to resist calling him. It took nearly two hours to put the wagon together, including several attempts to connect the pull handle so it faced in the right direction. I brought the wagon home. I went upstairs and got Libro.

He stood on the street staring at the little red wagon with a look of absolute disdain. I picked him up and put him inside it, easier now because he was so thin. He jumped out and glared at me. I was reminded of myself, postsurgery, pushing away offers of helping hands. I was reaching to pick him up a second time when Libro shook his body and marched off up the street on his skinny legs—with a determined look in his eye.

Not long afterward, I asked the question, point blank, of the person I most trusted to give me an honest answer. The good doctor assured and reassured me that Libro was not going to get any better. I didn't need anyone to tell me Libro was not having any fun. He was sitting on the floor in Doctor K.'s office, in a room furnished with soft floor cushions instead of the cold steel medical apparatus. Although the room might have been used for conversations, like the one we were having, I was sure it was also a death chamber. Decisions came in a flood—we would end Libro's life, but we would do it at home, on his own bed, surrounded by everything he loved, and only after I had time to prepare myself.

I asked Dr. K. to tell me in detail what the "procedure" would be like, what to expect. Circumstances

conspired for Dr. K., who was about to take a trip to
Florida, to set a date for a week later. Unlike a lifetime
of joy in the presence of the doctor who called him
"my friend," on this day, Libro kept looking at the
door, eager to leave.

On the way home from the vet's office, I began to
plan a grand farewell. For a week, until Dr. K. returned
to do the deed, Libro could have anything he wanted
to eat. Steak. Smelly pig's ears. Pasta without olive oil.
I'd buy a dozen new toys. I'd sing to him. And I would
invite all the people who loved him, from the mailman
to the nun in the park, from his local dog-run pals and
all his neighbors to his wide circle of "aunties," to
come by, if they wished, and say good-bye.

As we crossed West End Avenue, I saw Mattie the
Portuguese spaniel and his person waiting to cross
the street.

"Say good-bye to Libro," I told the woman. Her
eyes teared up. Although our lives had gone in different directions since we were first friends, she knew
what I meant and she leaned over to kiss the top of
Libro's head. Neither Mattie nor Libro treated the
encounter as anything different from a quick-sniff
street-corner hello.

The next morning, Libro was frantic, walking in circles the way he had when he first came home with
me. Those were panic attacks, I was sure, the after-

math of whatever had transpired while he roamed Riverside Park, abandoned, waiting to find his person. This time, it was something else. He was dying. I could see he was dying. And he needed to pee. He went to the door, looked at me imploringly, but I didn't want him to die on the stairs or in the street.

"No," I said. "You can pee on the floor. Pee anywhere. I don't mind at all. It's OK."

He wouldn't.

"Come here, on your bed."

I lay on his bed with my arms open wide while he circled in the center of the living room, went to the door, and came back. Then I called Heather. She was home in Long Island, painting the ceiling of her house for its renters, who would take over when she moved to Savannah with Poco for a new teaching job. She'd known that Libro had a week left.

"He's dying," I said. "He's dying now. And he keeps trying to get out the door to pee."

Heather went and got a headset that allowed her to use both hands on the paint roller while she stayed on the telephone with me from then on. I put Libro on the couch as he panted hard and wiped his lips with a cool washcloth. I stared into his eyes and told him I was with him, I would never leave him. His body was shutting down, but his soul was still dancing merrily in his eyes.

I had the most peculiar expectation in the midst of agony: that Libro would unzip his dog suit—the dark fur that I teased him in hot weather should be turned in for cooler seersucker—and out would step a figure who looked like Yoda. This sage, wizened character would proceed to explain away all the mysteries: where Libro had lived before we found each other in the park; who his parents and siblings had been; how his leg had been injured; why he had chosen me.

No Yoda appeared.

Dying took a long time, longer than I expected it to. My feeling that Libro's mortal life ending in my arms was a thing of beauty and the fulfillment of all my promises began to wane. When it became clear that he was suffering and that he might go on suffering for some time, I called the vet's office. Doctor K. was at the airport, but his partner Dr. Raclyn came, with a little black bag and accompanied by two aides from the office carrying a body bag.

That night, I wrote to the friends who had played with him and walked him, sailed with him and interviewed him, loved him, and cared:

*The great adventure ended today, a Tuesday in late August. The little brown angel heard his doctor and me decide that after a whole hot summer of pain and weight loss and more medication and shots (his) and tears (mine), it was time to let him go. We three made a date for a week later, after the doc returned from vacation. I envisioned seven days and nights of friends (mine and his) coming to say good-bye, 7 days of steak and smelly pigs ears, then candles, incense, champagne (for Libro too) and peace. But I dreaded it.*

*As always, Libro took care of me. Once he knew I had faced up to living without him, I am convinced, he decided to spare me more grief. So he climbed on his bed the morning after the last vet visit and in my arms, he died.*

# 8

# All Messages Have (Not) Been Erased

*The timing of death, like the ending of a story,*
*gives a changed meaning to what preceded it.*
—Mary Catherine Bateson

P eople say the darndest things in the face of death. As the brown body bag with Libro inside it was carried out the door by the two aides and after I had finished screaming that it looked like a garbage bag, Dr. Raclyn packed up his kit, held me in a compassionate hug and whispered, "Don't be alone tonight."

Alone was all I wanted to be. There were times I passionately needed people, as the last months of

Libro's life had more than demonstrated, but this was not one of them. I had said all there was to say. I had done all there was to do. There was nothing left but ritual, honor, and memory.

It was midafternoon and mild for August, with a bright sun and a breeze off the river. The dog run was busy, the café beginning to empty out, the soccer fields silent. I walked south, turning through the underpass where West Side Highway traffic echoed overhead until I was at the Hudson, then north along a path that led to the George Washington Bridge. I could not remember the last time I had been in the park, at the dog run, the café, or near the soccer fields without Libro beside me, but the rocks running along the river's edge were his most favorite place. Water-averse though he was, he was surefooted as a billy goat on those uneven rocks and fascinated by the debris that hid in their crevices. Bottles and cans, condoms, pages ripped from notebooks—he had found them all. Grudgingly, he would lie beside me in places where the rocks flattened, keeping one eye on the slowly moving river and bearing up under hot sun while I sunbathed, read, or dreamed into a notebook.

I'd walked more than a mile, less surefooted than Libro on the slippery stones, when I heard the dog panting. I turned to see nothing there. The sound continued, right behind me, close at my heels. I couldn't tell what small canine had followed me, breathing hard through its mouth and ducking out of sight when I looked back. I'd have to catch him out and carry him to the police station. Surely it was a "him."

The dog who wasn't there stayed with me, panting away, until the sun was sitting atop the buildings on the Jersey shore. On my walk home, retracing my steps, he and the sound of his breathing were gone. Was it Libro? I didn't even ask until weeks later.

After their beloved animals die, people also do the darndest things. A friend's tiny Maltese died in her bed before dawn. She and her husband wrapped the dog's body in a towel, put her in a wooden wine crate and stored her in the bar refrigerator to preserve her body (during the summer) until they could bury her near their country place over the weekend. For days, the couple had a wake when they finished work, "strong martinis over our cold hard doggie's body," she said. And "the real question wasn't whether to put her *in* the fridge . . . but whether to take her *out* every night at cocktail hour."

Dr. Raclyn had been right to assure me that I was lucky; Libro had died during working hours. Outside of cities, nobody needs to be called. Heather had carried Boo to her yard and buried him there. New York City rules prohibited using the parks as cemeteries, though I did wish Libro's body could be returned to the spot in Riverside Park where he had found me. I made stealth visits to the place, contemplating the fate of the ashes that would be coming.

I heard about a man whose golden retriever was killed on the road by a passing truck. The person who told me the story went to visit that man a few days later and lo and behold, there was a golden retriever, looking exactly like the dead one, sitting on the door-step. "*Sssh*," warned the man's wife, "I went the day af-ter the golden died and got another exactly like her. We've never spoken about it."

A lot of folks get a new dog or cat immediately. I couldn't. Some complain that friends and family fail to understand the grief or commiserate with the griever because it was "only a pet." I didn't think that would be a problem. Libro had admirers all over the neighborhood and well beyond it, too. In fact, soon after I informed those who were grouped in my e-mail address book as "Friends of Libro," I began receiving condolence notes and, later, actual cards, which I saved; though it pained me no end that he wasn't around to see how many lives he had touched and how very much he was loved. And he did adore an audience.

It was not uncommon to hear about the animal's spirit making itself felt to its people. A brush of fur across a hand. The sound of footsteps in an empty room. A lick on the face in the middle of the night. Days, months, years after the life had ended. Folklore is full of such tales. Rationalists say those "sightings" are imaginings; spiritualists swear by them. Willing to entertain the notion, I had no doubt if ever a spirit was strong enough to make its way through the barriers of the material world, it would be Libro's, but I was wrong. I looked. I listened. I sniffed. I waited. But aside from the panting dog in the park on the day he died, if that is what followed me, Libro never came back. A kabbalah scholar of my acquaintance insisted that souls migrate from one corporeal form to another until they are "done" and that the act of sheltering a soul on its last journey was sacred. Perhaps Libro was "done." I had no doubt about the sacred.

There was a lot of real world business to be done. My housecleaning, including the oil-splattered walls, became frenetic, like a Victorian maid airing out a sickroom after a death in the family. It took longer than reasonable for me to remove his fluffy dog bed— because his scent remained. But I'd been known to malinger the same way with pillowcases departed lovers had slept on. I sent his red Christmas stocking decorated with pearly white dog bones to Heather and Poco in Savannah, who actually celebrated Christmas. Kaya got his favorite rope pull toy and the set of raised stainless-steel food bowls I had bought near the end, when eating or drinking from dishes placed on the floor was painful for Libro. Kaya loved the toy and hated the bowls. Trixie got a basket full of three different kinds of shampoos, ear cleaner, breath freshener, something to stop a bleeding cut, and toothpaste. She ignored the cosmetics and grabbed Libro's ratty white bear, which she held in her teeth and shook violently. Olga and I agreed never to mention where it had come from. I did not know a dog who could use— perhaps, who deserved—the purple fleece winter coat, so I packed that away in a drawer. I kept his yellow life jacket and studded leather collar as acts of hope for the future.

In Riverside Park, in the same spot that his book celebration had been held nine years before, we had a party—a wake, perhaps—certainly a celebration. This time, it had nothing to do with book people, only dogs. The Alpha Dog band played again and Lowell Martin, the bandleader, dedicated a special piece for Libro. The Friends of Libro, including Eddie the mailman, Olga and Trixie, people from the dog run whose names I never knew, the owner of the red wagon, a man whose dachshund had just died, who could not stop weeping, assembled and drank and danced. Like any tribe, we celebrated Libro's life by sitting around the outdoor tables looking at the Hudson and telling stories about him. How he'd run to a neighbor's house when a rainstorm scared him. The times he sat for babies on the street. How he understood *siéntate* and *levántate* and even "good boy" in Spanish. His passion for the General Store in the Hamptons and his hatred for the water. Rocky's person told about the poodle's enlarged member that would not shrink. In the telling, many stories got better and better, embroidered by commentary.

My favorite story took place on the book tour, when I was reading in a bookstore. Libro was at my feet and suddenly stood up, prompting all the dogs in the room to bark, beginning in the front row and moving through the room, like a wave in the audience at a rock concert or a baseball game. This time, though, telling the story, picturing it, I realized that there was some communication going on between Libro and the dogs that I hadn't even thought about at the time. Was he saying "Look at me, I'm the dog in the book"? And were they responding with recognition or telling him to get over himself? Or was he acting like the interpreter who uses sign language for those in the audience who cannot hear? Was he translating the words of his person into something his fellow and sister dogs could understand? I'd never know. There would always be mysteries.

Libro's postmortem party ended with several local politicians making short speeches—we were closing in on another election. I made a speech, too. Others offered toasts. The band played. He would have loved it.

For a year after Libro died, my greatest joys were small, daily ones: the garden, the friends, the books read and the books in the process of being written, the ability to breathe in and breathe out, to walk the planet in sound health, to travel and to see two movies back-to-back without having to rush home by five. I hated the empty apartment and the silence that greeted me when I did come home and never stopped opening the door carefully, as though a creature with amber eyes and a set of paws might be waiting just inside. I avoided the dog run. I lost track of the neighborhood.

I felt widowed. No built-in Saturday-night date. No cocked head listening intently to my reading from new pages as they rolled off the printer. No bodyguard. No exterminator. Nobody to share the giggles of David Sedaris or the gasps of Dorothy Sayers with, or to scoff with me at the stupidity, at best, of television news. I slept alone. I shopped only for myself. Touch—hugs, kisses, strokes, even accidentally brushing against one another—was sharply diminished. I lived through Hurricane Katrina, which trapped Dr. K in Florida, and the November elections, without Libro to share it with. There was no one to whom I could say with conviction, "I will never leave you."

Did it matter much that my version of the intimacy and telepathic communication that had existed between myself and Libro might only be real in my imagination? That I might have invented it? One school of experts claims that dogs do what they do in our homes only because they need to be fed by us— and that we supply the rest, the illusions of understanding intimacy and love. I doubt it. With all my heart, I doubt it. And I don't think it matters at all.

Not only was I a widow, in my version, but an aging one as well, in anyone's version. What had seemed a fine, daring, liberated, fancy-free life before Libro came along had lost some of its luster. Not all, but some. Solitude still had its joys. Independence was nothing to be scoffed at. That was the beauty of choice, making a different one when the sun came up the next day or the next year. Now I was in that place, but trolling bars for nighttime company hardly appealed, nor did speed-dating or finding romance on a street corner, although a street corner might well be where a new dog might find me.

He came unsought and unbidden and he was not a dog, nor was he exactly new. A *hello* from long, long ago, across the threshold of my altar, my computer, in an e-mail. A distant wave from college days, an amiability with my younger self, long before serious writing, long before sanity, longer still before the pleasures of animal companionship. A fellow traveler he seemed, a lover of books and a magician of words and yet, as the correspondence became correspondence—like and unalike, male and female he made them both—paths

crossing in the oddest places, words crossing with un-
canny frequency—"ruminate," we each wrote and two
"ruminates" passed electronically and saluted, probably
over Kansas. Then "enjoy."

We ruminated, we enjoyed, and each admitted it
seemed in chronological time that we had arrived si-
multaneously at the beginning of Act V of our life-
times. What would it be? How would it read? We sent
photos. His—handsome, still, perhaps more handsome as a man with a history now than the insouciant
college boy I remembered—was pasted near my magic
writing machinery, close to the container that now
held Libro's ashes. My men—one now gone, one to
come. Auguries were impossible to resist:

"You know who sent him?" said Ann, a connois-
seur of the art of divination.

I was afraid she would say "God," but she said "Libro," and we indulged for some time in the specula-
tion that from Doggy Heaven, if it existed, the little
brown angel had been *tsk-tsk*ing. He'd taught me love,
and what had I done with the lesson since his departure? Ruminated. Became introspective. Sat at my
desk, typing away. No kisses. No embraces. No eye
contact or soul-connection. Not good.

Here's a chance.

I let the handsome, graying chance cross my threshold
with less resistance than I had let Libro do the same

a decade before. Unlike Libro, this was no puppy, this one had lived as long as I had and it had not been un-blemished. Though Libro's gimpiness showed from the first week we lived together, the man's hurt was not visible as he came through the door. When we spoke and touched, it was.

He went away. For a while, he wrote notes, but they were notes in a different voice, small and tight and not smile-inducing. The notes dribbled away into mere sentences, fragments, and then a period like the one at the end of this sentence.

I picked up my life, a bit the worse for broken hope and wear.

Weeks later, I heard footsteps on the stairs. It was Linda, the newly rescued dark brown pit mix who looked more like a deer than a dog, with Alex and Marilu, my Chilean neighbors. I opened the door. Linda wore Libro's purple fleece winter coat, which had fit him snugly, like a muscle shirt, but flapped around young Linda's legs.

"*Hola*, Linda," I said. "*¿Como estas? Siéntate.*" She sat. I let her kiss my face.

"You are my stepdog," I said, in English, not know-ing a Spanish word for stepdog. Families, in English or Spanish, come in surprising designs.

I went back to work at my desk. In the building, water was running, people were coming and going, pots were banging, a radio was playing. When this building went up at the end of the nineteenth century in what was then a country suburb of Manhattan, there were two ways of being a dog here. If you were a rich dog, you sat daintily on a lady's lap or hunted with the master. If you were poor, you worked or tried to survive in the streets. There were no lives like Libro's then, nor like mine. Ladies were known for their pale complexions, lack of exertion, and need for protection. Working women had no time to cavort with canines, nor would it have pleased many of them to do so. Ours was a story not only romantic and urban, but modern.

Or postmodern, where the final curtain never comes down.

Like Libro hearing the phone ring seconds before it actually rang, or like the animals of Asia moving to higher ground before the tsunami crashed ashore, I sensed something about to happen, the story going on. What now?

My nose twitched, trying to smell the future. I typed these words:

*A book, a dog, or a man.*

*A man, a dog, or a book.*